KELLY FITZSIMMONS BURTON

Reason and Proper Function
A Response to Alvin Plantinga

Public Philosophy Press

First published by Public Philosophy Press 2019

Copyright © 2019 by Kelly Fitzsimmons Burton

All rights reserved. No part of this publication may be reproduced, stored or transmitted in any form or by any means, electronic, mechanical, photocopying, recording, scanning, or otherwise without written permission from the publisher. It is illegal to copy this book, post it to a website, or distribute it by any other means without permission.

Cover design by Beth Ellen Nagle

www.publicphilosophypress.com

First edition

ISBN: 978-0-578-50024-9

This book was professionally typeset on Reedsy. Find out more at reedsy.com

For those wrestling with skepticism

Contents

Foreword	ii
Preface	v
Acknowledgement	vii
Justification Described And Denied	1
Warrant Described	17
Warrant Denied	29
Bibliography	77
Also by Kelly Fitzsimmons Burton	79

Foreword

Approximately 20 years ago, as a graduate student in philosophy at Arizona State University, I was struggling intensely with the problem of skepticism. Skepticism is the philosophical position that knowledge is not possible, that nobody can really know for sure. The challenge of skepticism, at that time, came primarily through Edmund Gettier's counterexamples to the sufficiency of justification as the component that makes true belief into knowledge. Gettier examples are meant to show us that one may have justified true belief, and still lack knowledge. Perhaps some fourth condition in addition to justification and true belief was needed for knowledge. During my early graduate school training, I considered the gauntlet thrown down. I still believed that knowledge was possible, contra my strong skeptical training. And I still believed that justified true belief (JTB) was the correct path for obtaining knowledge.

My professors at ASU were very much aware of my struggle against the dominant skepticism of the day and encouraged me to read Alvin Plantinga as a possible solution to skepticism and a way to overcome Gettier's challenge to justified true belief as knowledge. Whereas Gettier questioned the sufficiency of the JTB formulation of knowledge, Plantinga questioned the necessity of the JTB formulation. Perhaps the traditional definition of knowledge is mistaken and should be reconsidered?

Plantinga proposes that knowledge is warranted true belief, where a belief is warranted if it is formed by cognitive faculties functioning properly in an appropriate environment, according to a good design plan. He shifts the terms of the discussion from an internalist view of justification to an externalist view of warrant. I read all of Plantinga's works on epistemology, which were very recent at the time of my studies, with the anticipation that he would provide a way out of Gettier's skeptical implications. What I found instead was another form of skepticism, a religious form of skepticism, which we can term fideism. I did not focus on Plantinga's fideism, but my good friend Owen Anderson did in his work *The Clarity Of God's Existence: The Ethics of Belief After the Enlightenment* (Oregon: Wipf & Stock, 2008). Instead, I took a critical look at one aspect of Plantinga's formulation of warrant, that of "proper function," which is the key piece of his externalist account of knowledge.

This short work is my early attempt at defending the traditional JTB account of knowledge. The substance of the work is my original master's thesis. Since I first wrote this thesis, I have written further on the topic of overcoming skepticism by understanding what knowledge is by understanding what is involved in justification. An in depth defense of knowledge may be found in my recent book *Retrieving Knowledge: A Socratic Response to Skepticism* (Phoenix: Public Philosophy Press, 2018).

My hope in publishing this book is that future graduate students in philosophy will not have to undergo the same intense, and somewhat needless, struggle with skepticism resulting from the Gettier problem and from Plantinga's response that I had to undergo. Skepticism leads to cynicism and nihilism, which are contrary to the pursuit of knowledge, the fruit of philosophy. If philosophy is to survive, knowledge of reality must be possible. I heartily believe that knowledge is possible and want to encourage all who read this book to pursue knowledge as the highest end.

Preface

Alvin Plantinga, in *Warrant: The Current Debate*, notes that there is a long history in Anglo-American epistemology that traces back to the classical internalist views of Rene Descartes and John Locke. Internalism is the view that an individual has special access to that quantity or quality that makes true belief into knowledge. This internalism, according to Plantinga, is motivated by deontology – or epistemic duty fulfillment. Closely connected with epistemic deontology is justification. Justification (or what Plantinga prefers to call 'warrant') is that quantity or quality, enough of which makes true belief into knowledge. Plantinga strongly objects to the deontological view of justification, claiming that no amount of duty fulfillment can get us to knowledge. He says justification is neither necessary nor sufficient for warrant.

In *Warrant: The Current Debate* (hereafter WCD) Plantinga examines several versions of internalism – from Classical and Post-Classical Chisholmian internalism, several forms of coherentism, to reliablism – to show that none of these views get us to that quantity or quality enough of which makes true belief into knowledge. Plantinga rejects all of these views, arguing that what is needed is a view that takes into account the proper function of our cognitive faculties. He then proposes to give a more accurate account of warrant in *Warrant and Proper Function* (WPF). Plantinga's theory is that a belief is warranted if it is formed by cognitive faculties functioning properly in an appropriate environment and according to a good design plan.

The purpose of this book is to examine Plantinga's view of cognitive malfunction in connection with his view of warrant and his rejection of the traditional view of justification. I will argue that the cognitive faculty of reason does not and cannot malfunction in the way that Plantinga either explicitly or implicitly suggests. Consequently Plantinga's criticism of justification does not stand. I argue further that if reason is not subject to malfunction and is thus reliable, the traditional view of justification – having appropriate reasons for belief in conjunction with true belief, possibly with the addition of a fourth condition (the carefulness criterion) – will get us to knowledge.

Acknowledgement

I would like to thank and acknowledge Dr. Surrendra Gangadean, my first philosophy professor, mentor, and friend, who introduced me to the good life. I would also like to acknowledge the friendship and camaraderie of Dr. Owen Anderson, who was there in the early days of grad school and is still there now.

Without my professors at Arizona State University, this work would not have taken the shape that it did. I thank Dr.'s Stephen Reynolds, Steward Cohen, and Bernard Kobes for challenging me to think critically and for chairing my original thesis committee.

I acknowledge my students over 16 years of teaching and the daily challenges that they pose with their probing questions, doubt, and sometimes embrace of the good.

Lastly, I thank my husband, David, who is a constant partner in pursuit of what is true, good, and beautiful.

1

Justification Described And Denied

Alvin Plantinga, philosopher in the area of epistemology, explains contemporary, Anglo-American views of justification in light of the classical internalist views of Rene Descartes and John Locke. He believes that, prior to Descartes, externalism was the dominant epistemic view, going back at least to Aristotle. With Descartes' *Meditations* internalism came to the forefront and has dominated the Western tradition since. Plantinga objects to internalism in an effort to return to an externalist view. Externalism is the position, which claims that an individual does not always have special access to those things that confer warrant on a belief.

Setting the Stage

What is this internalist tradition and what are its components that Plantinga ultimately rejects? Plantinga believes that there are three main components to what he deems "classical deontological internalism." These include epistemic deontology, or the notion that "we have epistemic duties or obligations." Epistemic deontology "induces internalism," which is the second component to warrant. "And the central duty . . . is to believe a proposition that is not certain only on the basis of evidence"[1] which is justification. The elements involved in classical deontological internalism then are epistemic deontology, internalism, and justification. Plantinga states that:

> *Justification, internalism, and epistemic deontology are properly seen as a closely related triumvirate: internalism flows from deontology and is unmotivated without it, and justification is at bottom and originally a deontological notion.[2]*

Internalism is the view that a person can always be aware of some internal epistemic state that confers warrant on a belief. An example of this state may be determining by reflection alone whether I have a reason for belief, or possibly whether a belief is certain. Internalism is the view that a person has special access to what confers justification for belief, or the ground of justification, and this state is internal to that person. A person may "determine by *reflection alone* whether a belief has warrant for him."[3] For example, according to the internalist view, a person may by reflection alone determine whether he has adequate reasons for believing the truth of a proposition. Plantinga believes that epistemic internalism plays a central role in most views of justification.

Plantinga claims that the source of internalism as an epistemic notion is epistemic justification. The traditional view of knowledge is that knowledge is justified true belief. Up until Edmund Gettier's landmark essay: "Is Justified True Belief Knowledge?"[4] true belief, with the addition of justification, was regarded as necessary and sufficient for knowledge. After Gettier's objections to the sufficiency of justification and true belief for knowledge, justification and true belief may be viewed as necessary and "nearly sufficient" for knowledge. But what exactly is justification?

Plantinga notes that there are several, seemingly confusing, notions of what justification is. But there are common features among the various views of justification. Justification involves "*epistemic responsibility*; a belief is justified if the person holding it is not guilty of epistemic irresponsibility in forming or maintaining it."[5] Epistemic responsibility involves the notion that the aim for one's believings is truth, and that a person will only accept beliefs which he "has good reason to think are true."[6] A second common feature in theories of justification is the close connection between justification and internalism.

Plantinga's view is that "the believer must have cognitive access to . . . whether or not he is justified . . . or to the grounds of his justification."[7] According to the internalist this access must somehow be internal to the cognizer and the cognizer from this special access can determine by reflection alone whether he has adequate reasons for a particular belief to be justified. Lastly, Plantinga notes that many views hold that "justification is a matter of *having evidence*, or at least depends upon evidence."[8] This evidence need not necessarily be empirical evidence, but may include evidence based upon reason. Justification involves having a reason, or having evidence, for a belief. In sum, justification is aimed at truth, and involves one's being epistemically responsible in the formation and maintenance of beliefs. Epistemic responsibility means that a person has adequate reasons or evidence for believing and maintaining that a belief is true. Justification is what almost makes true belief into knowledge, and it is an internally accessible epistemic state.

Plantinga questions the relationship between justification and evidence. He asks, "how does it happen that justification is associated, in this way, with evidence? And what is the source of the internalist requirement, and how does it fit in? And why is justification associated, in this way, with knowledge?"[9] To answer these questions, Plantinga believes that we need to explore yet a third component to internalist justification, that is, deontology. Deontology in an epistemic sense is a normative notion. It implies duty, and possibly moral obligation. Deontology in this context involves doing one's epistemic duty or fulfilling one's epistemic obligations. One's epistemic duty or obligation may be to abstain from believing something for which one has insufficient evidence or believing a proposition only on the basis of sufficient evidence. Deontology has to do with one "regulating" one's beliefs according to the evidence one has. Plantinga sums up epistemic deontology in the following way, "[it is] the thought that being justified in holding a belief is having fulfilled one's epistemic duties in forming or continuing to hold that belief . . ."[10]

Plantinga traces the notion of epistemic deontology back to the epistemological views of Rene Descartes and John Locke, whom he deems "the fountainheads of the tradition of classical internalism."[11] He notes that Descartes "thinks that one is justified only in accepting just those propositions that are clear and distinct [for one]."[12] It is one's duty to accept only the propositions which one perceives clearly and distinctly. Plantinga notes that Locke believes it is your epistemic duty to "regulate your beliefs in such a way that you believe a proposition only if you have good reason for it. . . ."[13] In other words, one ought not to believe a proposition that one does not have good reason for believing.

Plantinga believes that contemporary views of justification have their roots in the classical views of Descartes and Locke. He acknowledges, "classical deontological internalism has a certain deep integrity."[14] Yet, he notes that contemporary views, such as that of Roderick Chisholm, and "other contemporary accounts . . . sometimes seize on one or another of the elements of the classical package, often in such a way that the integrity of the original package is lost, or at least no longer clearly visible."[15] Plantinga respects certain aspects of classical deontological internalism though not agreeing with it. He is primarily opposed to contemporary views that emphasize one aspect, say duty fulfillment, or having adequate evidence, such that the classical view becomes distorted from its original conception. Plantinga raises objections to these contemporary views throughout *WCD* beginning with Roderick Chisholm's view.

From Classical to Contemporary Internalism

Now that we have an explanation of what justification is we may want to ask, along with Plantinga, whether "warrant . . . can be explained in terms of justification?"[16] Warrant is that quantity or quality enough of which makes true belief into knowledge. Plantinga ultimately denies that warrant may be explained in terms of justification. He argues that justification is neither necessary nor sufficient for warrant.

He objects to many versions of justification throughout *WCD*. In each case he uses a similar strategy. I shall focus primarily on his objections to the internalist view of Roderick Chisholm. Chisholm is an influential contemporary philosopher in epistemology. His view of justification is internalist and deontological and has its roots in the classical internalist views of Descartes and Locke. When examining Chisholm's view of justification it should be asked whether his view gives us that quantity or quality enough of which makes true belief into knowledge. Plantinga says no, let us find out why.

Chisholm does not make the same distinction between justification and warrant that Plantinga does. For Chisholm, the thing which makes true belief into knowledge is "positive epistemic status." Positive epistemic status has to do with the fulfillment of one's duty or obligation in relation to knowledge. Chisholm "sees warrant or positive epistemic status as essentially connected with *deontological epistemic justification*, the condition of having satisfied one's epistemic duties or obligations."[17] Chisholm suggests that we have a duty, as intellectual beings, to strive for "epistemic excellence," where epistemic excellence involves our attempting to stand in the right relation to the truth. Positive epistemic status is the fulfillment of epistemic duty. That duty involves our trying to achieve and maintain epistemic excellence. This condition of epistemic excellence is "a duty I have '*qua* intellectual being'- that is, just by virtue of being the sort of creature that is capable of grasping and believing (or withholding) propositions."[18]

Plantinga objects to the notion of epistemic duty and obligation, but moreover, he objects to the fact that one may try to bring about the condition of epistemic excellence. He states that, according to Chisholm, "my requirement is not to succeed in maintaining epistemic excellence; my requirement is only to *try* to do so."[19] How is it that an individual may try to bring about the conditions whereby he stands in the right relation to truth such that knowledge ensues? How does one achieve epistemic excellence, and is one obligated to do so? Plantinga claims that even though one may do one's epistemic best to stand in the right relation to truth, one may hold beliefs that lack warrant for one. I can do my epistemic best yet still lack justification and therefore not have knowledge. How is this so? Plantinga states that a person may have performed works of "epistemic supererogation" yet he may be deceived by a Cartesian demon, Alpha Centurion cognitive scientist, or have a brain lesion that may keep him from being in the right relation to truth and thus could lead to his belief's not having warrant for him. Plantinga claims that doing one's epistemic duty, plus true belief, is not sufficient for knowledge. Furthermore, he claims that neither are even necessary for knowledge. He uses very clever counterexamples to establish the basis of his objections. I will examine two of these counterexamples.

Justification not Sufficient for Warrant

Plantinga says "Taking 'justification' in its original and most natural sense," that is deontologically, "what I shall argue is that justification is wholly insufficient for warrant," and he adds, "it is also not necessary for it."[20] Deontological justification, as Plantinga understands it, "[is] working as hard as [one can] to achieve epistemic excellence,"[21] where epistemic excellence is close to being warrant. Epistemic excellence is a state of affairs that one works hard to bring about.

Plantinga spells out the implications of two of Chisholm's principles connected with epistemic excellence. He states that according to Chisholm, "a person perceptually takes there to be something that is F if he is appeared to in a certain way Z, believes that there is something that appears to him in way Z, and believes that that thing has the property of being F."[22] Secondly, he notes: "a proposition is beyond reasonable doubt for x just if believing that proposition is a pretty good way for x to fulfill his epistemic duty."[23] Plantinga argues that one may perceptually take there to be something that is F when appeared to in way Z but due to cognitive dysfunction or deception be mistaken in believing that what appears to him in way Z has the property of being F. For instance, he gives an example of Paul, an epistemically dutiful person who is deceived by a Cartesian demon, or has a brain lesion such that:

> *When Paul is aurally appeared to in the church-bell fashion, . . . he finds himself with a powerful, nearly ineluctable tendency or impulse to believe that there is something that is appearing to him in that fashion, and that thing is orange.*[24]

In this case Paul is appeared to aurally upon hearing a church-bell, and though doing his epistemic best in forming and maintaining his beliefs, due to cognitive deception or dysfunction he forms the belief that he is appeared to in the church-bell way. Believing that he is appeared to in the church-bell way and forming the belief that this thing is orange is beyond reasonable doubt for Paul because he believes that this is the best way for him to fulfill his epistemic duty.

Plantinga claims that there is a certain amount of 'positive epistemic status' that Paul's beliefs have when he is appeared to in the church-bell way and believes this thing he perceives is orange. These beliefs were "formed in accord with a serious and determined effort to live dutifully,"[25] but this is not the same as 'warrant'. He says:

> *Nevertheless there is also a kind of positive epistemic status this belief lacks for him, a kind crucial for knowledge: it lacks warrant. For that sort of positive epistemic status, it is not sufficient that one satisfy one's duty and do one's epistemic best. Paul can be so conscientious about his epistemic duties, and still be such that his beliefs have very little warrant. And the reason, fundamentally, is that even though he is doing his epistemic duty to the uttermost, his epistemic faculties are defective; this deprives the belief in question of any substantial degree of that quantity.[26]*

Paul's belief lacks warrant because though he does his epistemic best in forming and maintaining the belief that he is appeared to in the orange church-bell way when appeared to aurally by the sound of church bells, it is not the case that the church-bell actually is orange. He holds this false belief due to cognitive deception or dysfunction.

Epistemic duty is the essence of justification according to Plantinga, yet epistemic duty or excellence may not get us to warrant, that quantity or quality enough of which makes true belief knowledge. Plantinga concludes that deontological justification is not sufficient for warrant. One may do one's epistemic duty, that is, be justified, and yet have cognitive faculties that malfunction, such that a belief lacks warrant. Therefore, "no degree of dutifulness, no amount of living up to one's obligations and satisfying one's responsibilities - in a word, no degree of justification - can be sufficient for warrant."[27]

Justification not Necessary for Warrant

We have seen Plantinga's argument against the sufficiency of justification for warrant, through the example of the epistemically dutiful Paul. Yet Plantinga makes the stronger claim that justification is not necessary for warrant. Plantinga argues this point by means of a counterexample, which I will quote almost in full. He argues:

> *Suppose there is the sort of epistemic duty Chisholm suggests: a duty to try to bring it about that I attain and maintain the condition of epistemic excellence; and suppose I know this, am dutiful, but also a bit confused. I come nonculpably to believe that our Alpha Centurion conquerors, for reasons opaque to us, thoroughly dislike my thinking that I am perceiving something that is red; I also believe that they are monitoring my beliefs and, if I form the belief that I see something red, will bring it about that I have a set of beliefs most of which are absurdly false, thus depriving me of any chance for epistemic excellence. I thereby acquire an epistemic duty to try to withhold the beliefs I naturally form when I am appeared to redly: such beliefs as that I see a red ball or a fire engine, or whatever. Of course I have the same epistemic inclinations everyone else has: when I am appeared to redly, I am powerfully inclined to believe that I see something that is red. By dint of heroic and unstinting effort, however, I am able to train myself to withhold the belief (on such occasions) that I see something red; naturally it takes enormous effort and requires great willpower . . . I am appeared to redly in a particularly insistent and out-and-out fashion by*

> *a large red London bus. "Epistemic duty be hanged," I mutter, and relax blissfully into the belief that I am now perceiving something red. Then this would be a belief that was unjustified for me; in accepting it I would be going contrary to epistemic duty; yet could it not constitute knowledge nonetheless?[28]*

In this counterexample I believe it is my epistemic duty, while maintaining my overall set of beliefs, to refrain from believing that I am being appeared to redly. Yet, the Alpha Centurions who monitor my beliefs dislike my believing that I am appeared to redly. When I do believe that I am appeared to redly they will bring it about that I have "a set of beliefs most of which are absurdly false,"[29] and thus I will fail to be in the right relation to truth, which is my epistemic duty. So instead of believing that I am appeared to redly when it seems that I am, "[I] try to withhold the beliefs I naturally form when I am appeared to redly."[30] I take withholding this belief to be my epistemic duty. When I can no longer maintain the duty of withholding belief that I am appeared to redly when it seems that I am, and out of sheer exhaustion I believe that I see a big red London bus, when I actually do, then I am flouting my epistemic duty to withhold belief when I am appeared to redly. Yet when I do see the big red London bus, it really is there, and I do know this. Therefore, I have flouted my epistemic duty. I have gone against my duty in believing the bus is red, and in addition I may actually have knowledge according to Plantinga.

The counterexample that Plantinga uses to show that justification, i.e. duty, is not necessary for warrant is supposed to show that we can fail to do our duty and yet still arrive at knowledge. What Plantinga is aiming for in his counterexamples is the need for proper function, or the notion that one can be ever so dutiful, yet because of cognitive malfunction, fail to have justification for belief. He says:

> *The conclusion to be drawn, I think, is that justification properly so-called - deontological justification - is not so much as necessary for warrant. Justification is a fine thing, a valuable state of affairs - intrinsically as well as extrinsically; but it is neither necessary nor sufficient for warrant. Chisholm's powerful and powerfully developed versions of deontological internalism - classical Chisholmian internalism - must be rejected.[31]*

Justification is not necessary for a belief to be warranted. We must look elsewhere.

Duty as the Central Notion of Justification

Plantinga's counterexamples throughout *WCD* are primarily objections to the notion of duty in justification. He argues that no matter how hard one tries to do one's duty, one may still not be justified because one's cognitive faculties may be malfunctioning, or one may be deceived by a Cartesian demon, Alpha Centurion cognitive scientist, I may be a brain-in-a-vat, etc.. But should doing one's epistemic duty be singled out as the central concept in justification? Is it *the* central concept of justification?

In fact, one does have an obligation, or duty, to give reasons or have evidence for one's belief. The central notion to justification is having reasons for belief. If one does not have appropriate reasons for one's belief, there is a lack of justification. Duty may be a secondary notion of justification. It may be our duty as intellectual beings to give reasons for our beliefs and have reasons in order to be justified. But the central notion of justification is giving reasons, not duty. Laurence BonJour, a contemporary philosopher supports this view and states:

> . . . *Knowledge requires the satisfaction of two distinct conditions in addition to belief and truth. The third condition, for which the term "justification" is most standardly employed, has to do with the presence of something like a reason or ground for the truth or likely truth of the belief.[32]*

There is no indication of duty fulfillment as a requirement for justification in BonJour's definition, yet he does note the requirement of a reason or ground for the truth of a belief. Another contemporary, Ernest Sosa, speaking of the deontological element of justification, notes:

> *My main problem is . . . that of whether this notion of "epistemic justification" captures an epistemic status of primary interest to epistemology, even to "internalists" generally. Don't we fall short in our effort to throw light on internalist epistemic justification if we stop with . . . explicated deontological justification. . . ?[33]*

He adds further "one could secure internalism, and define a sort of "epistemic justification" even without invoking the full deontological machinery."[34] I interpret Sosa to be saying that it is possible to have a theory of internalist justification that is not primarily based upon epistemic deontology.

Lastly, though not particularly agreeing with the position, Richard Foley notes, "Being justified in believing a proposition P is typically thought of as an internal condition; it is a matter of the believer having, or being able to construct, an argument for P."[35] Constructing an argument for P would involve having reasons for P and not particularly fulfilling some epistemic duty. These quotes are intended to show that one may hold to a view of internalist justification and yet hold to deontology as a secondary and less central notion of justification. What these quotes also support is the notion that having a reason, evidence, or argument for belief is the main concept of justification.

Counterexamples and Contemporary Views

Plantinga believes that his objections to Classical Chisholmian Internalism, and the view of justification that goes along with it, hold against all forms of deontological justification, for he says:

> *I argued that in the twentieth century received tradition in Anglo-American epistemology - a tradition going back at least to Locke - sees justification as essentially deontological but also necessary and nearly sufficient (sufficient up to Gettier) for warrant. Although this is an attractive, indeed, a seductive approach to an understanding of warrant, it is nevertheless at bottom deeply flawed. No amount of dutifulness, epistemic or otherwise, is sufficient for warrant.[36]*

Plantinga objects to other versions of internalism, namely various forms of coherentism, and then he objects to reliabilism, using similar counterexamples as those cited above. He argues against each version of internalism individually, making the point in each case that justification is not necessary or sufficient for warrant. He uses counterexamples that show a person may do his epistemic best but not arrive at knowledge because of some cognitive malfunction. What is needed, he argues, is an account of warrant that guarantees the proper function of one's cognitive faculties. I shall turn briefly to consider the view of warrant that Plantinga proposes as an alternative to both the classical and contemporary views of justification.

[1]Plantinga, Alvin. *Warrant the Current Debate*. (New York: Oxford University Press, 1993), 28.
  [2]Ibid., 29.
  [3]Ibid., 5.
  [4]Gettier, Edmund. "Is Justified True Belief Knowledge?" *Analysis*. Vol. 23 No. 6 (1963): 121-123.
  [5]Plantinga, *WCD*, 10.
  [6]BonJour, Laurence. qtd in Plantinga, *WCD*, 8.
  [7]Ibid., 10.
  [8]Ibid.
  [9]Ibid., 11.
  [10]Ibid., 14.
  [11]Ibid., 11.
  [12]Ibid., 14.
  [13]Ibid.
  [14]Ibid., 28.
  [15]Ibid.

[16]Ibid., 29.
[17]Ibid., 30.
[18]Ibid., 33.
[19]Ibid.
[20]Ibid., 36.
[21]Ibid., 42.
[22]Ibid., 41.
[23]Ibid.
[24]Ibid., 42.
[25]Ibid.
[26]Ibid., 43.
[27]Ibid.
[28]Ibid., 45.
[29]Ibid.
[30]Ibid.
[31]Ibid.

[32]Kvanvig, Jonathan. *Warrant in Contemporary Epistemology*. (Maryland: Rowman & Littlefield Publishers, Inc., 1996), 49.

[33]Ibid., 81.
[34]Ibid.
[35]Ibid., 88.
[36]Platinga, *WCD*, 45-46.

2

Warrant Described

In the previous chapter we examined Alvin Plantinga's rejection of both the classical and contemporary views of deontological justification. In rejecting these views Plantinga does not leave us high and dry without an explanation of that quantity or quality enough of which makes true belief into knowledge. Instead he proposes an alternative explanation in his book, *Warrant and Proper Function* (hereafter *WPF*). He calls this alternative account of that quantity or quality "warrant". He stipulates that it is warrant plus true belief that constitutes knowledge. This chapter will serve as a brief exploration of Plantinga's view of warrant and the conditions which he believes make true belief into knowledge.

The "First Approximation" of Warrant

I will begin by examining in general the four conditions necessary for warrant. Plantinga states:

> *(1) A necessary condition of a belief's having warrant for me is that my cognitive equipment, my belief-forming and belief-maintaining apparatus or powers, be free of . . . malfunction. A belief has warrant for you only if your cognitive apparatus is functioning properly, working the way it ought to work, in producing and sustaining [belief].*[1]

Plantinga says, "the notion of proper function . . . is presupposed by the idea of functional generalizations."[2] By "functional generalizations" Plantinga means "how human beings or other organisms or their parts and organs function: how they work, what their purposes are, and how they react under various circumstances."[3] Functional generalizations contain the notion of proper function. Proper function is a notion that we all have, and it is seen in things like a person's thyroid properly functioning, or a bird's wing properly functioning. Whereas, if these things malfunction the person with a dysfunctional thyroid will need thyroid medication to regulate the thyroid. Or the bird with a malfunctioning wing will not be able to fly until it is corrected or healed. Plantinga notes that on the face of it proper function is a common sense notion. He believes that we all have it. He says, "let us provisionally entertain the idea that a belief has warrant for me only if the relevant parts of my noetic equipment – the parts involved in its formation and sustenance - are functioning properly."[4]

Plantinga thinks that more is needed besides proper function in order to have warrant for a belief. For we may have perfectly working cognitive faculties but be in an environment not suited for those faculties and our beliefs may lack warrant. Therefore "another component to warrant" is that: "(2) . . . your faculties must be in good working order, and the environment must be appropriate for your particular repertoire of epistemic powers. It must be the sort of environment for which your faculties are designed - by God or evolution (or both)."[5] The environment in which our cognitive faculties function must be the appropriate one for those faculties. It may be that Alpha Centauri is not an environment suitable for our cognitive faculties in which case our beliefs may lack warrant in this environment.

Plantinga suggests that beliefs come in degrees, and though my cognitive faculties may be functioning properly in an appropriate environment one belief may have more by way of warrant for me than another. For example, I may believe that *1+2 =3* more strongly than I believe something that occurred in the distant past, say that I had a red bicycle when I was 8 years old. He states that "when my faculties are functioning properly, a belief has warrant to the degree that I find myself inclined to accept it; and this (again, if my faculties are functioning properly and nothing interferes) will be the degree to which I *do* accept it."[6] He suggests that we find ourselves believing, it is not something we do, but is something that happens to us, and the more inclined we are to believing something, the more warrant that belief has for us, that is, if our faculties are functioning properly.

Plantinga writes: "the proposed condition for warrant - proper function in an appropriate environment - isn't anywhere nearly sufficient for warrant."[7] He says there may be cases where our cognitive faculties function properly in an appropriate environment and yet they may still lack warrant. They may lack warrant because the part of the design plan that produced the belief may be aimed at something other than truth. For example, "someone may remember a painful experience as less painful than it was, as is sometimes said to be the case with childbirth."[8] The remembrance of a painful experience as less painful than it actually was is not a belief that is aimed at truth, yet it may have some other purpose within our cognitive makeup. Beliefs such as wish fulfillment, and possibly some religious beliefs, may fall within the category of beliefs not aimed at truth. These beliefs, though formed by cognitive faculties functioning properly in an appropriate environment, lack warrant because they are not aimed at truth but "are instead aimed at something else . . .."[9] He concludes that something more is needed for warrant.

Plantinga proposes the 'design plan' as a third component of warrant. He says, "the design plan for human beings will include specifications for our *cognitive* system or faculties."[10] A design plan is something like a blueprint, or specifications, as to how a thing ought to work. He says concerning the third condition: "(3) What confers warrant is one's cognitive faculties working properly, or working according to the design plan *insofar as that segment of the design plan is aimed at producing true beliefs.*"[11] The relevant "segment" of the design plan is that part of our cognitive system that leads us to true beliefs, as opposed to wish fulfillment, survival, the memory of painful experiences as less painful, etc., which are not aimed at true belief but at something else.

These three conditions, according to Plantinga, are still not sufficient for warrant. He believes that the design plan must also be a good one. So, he adds yet a fourth condition to warrant. He notes:

> *(4) The design plan must be a good one - more exactly, that the design governing the production of the belief in question is a good one; Still more exactly, that the objective probability of a belief's being true, given that it is produced by cognitive faculties functioning in accord with the relevant module of the design plan, is high.[12]*

Plantinga sums up an approximation of the conditions of warrant, without claiming them to be a "neat formula" or a "short and snappy list of conditions . . . that are severally necessary and jointly sufficient for warrant."[13] He suggests that his formula is vague and that there probably is no succinct and accurately definable set of conditions for warrant. Yet he gives his definition:

> *To a first approximation, we may say that a belief B has warrant for S if and only if the relevant segments [of the design plan] (the segments involved in the production of B) are functioning properly in a cognitive environment sufficiently similar to that for which S's faculties are designed; and the modules of the design plan governing the production of B are (1) aimed at truth, and (2) such that there is a high objective probability that a belief formed in accordance with those modules (in that sort of cognitive*

> *environment) is true; and the more firmly* S *believes* B *the more warrant* B *has for* S.*[14]*

He gives a definition of warrant and then says, "this is at best a first approximation; it is still at most programmatic, a suggestion, an idea, a hint."[15] Now that we have a "first approximation" of warrant, maybe it would be appropriate to examine the individual conditions of warrant in greater detail.

A More Detailed Account

I would like to examine in greater detail the conditions for warrant that Plantinga proposes. These include proper function, cognitive environment, and the design plan. In the following chapter I will ask whether these conditions are necessary or sufficient for warrant, and furthermore whether warrant is sufficient for knowledge. But first, let us examine the nuts and bolts of warrant itself.

Proper Function

When describing proper function, Plantinga often compares our cognitive faculties to the proper function of organs in the body or to mechanical objects - such as an automobile. He claims that we all have a notion of proper function that we understand and adopt in our everyday lives. We know proper function in a sort of common sense way. A thing is functioning properly if it does what it is supposed to do. It is malfunctioning if it is not doing what it is supposed to. My watch is functioning properly if it accurately keeps the time. It is malfunctioning if it does not keep time accurately. My eyes function properly if they produce 20/20 vision. If I happen to have cataracts my eyes are not functioning properly. My computer functions properly only if there are no bugs or viruses in the programming. We now have an idea of proper function from everyday usage. This common sense notion of proper function is supposed to carry over, according to Plantinga, to understanding the proper function of our cognitive faculties.

Proper function of our cognitive faculties must first rule out the influences of any outsiders such as Alpha Centurion cognitive scientists, Cartesian evil demons, and also internal influences such as a brain lesion or even the influence of mind-altering substances. All of these influences may cause one's faculties to fail to function properly. What is proper function, positively? This point seems a little unclear. It appears that proper function of our cognitive faculties just means that "there is nothing wrong with your cognitive faculties; they are working quite properly."[16]

What exactly does it mean for our cognitive faculties to properly function? Does a cognizer ever have good reason to believe that *his* faculties are functioning properly? The notion of proper function, on the face of it, seems very plain, very straightforward. Yet, when it is applied to our cognitive faculties it soon becomes unclear. By proper function, does Plantinga have in mind such things as that I am fully awake and alert while reasoning? Would an example of my cognitive faculties failing to function properly in ordinary daily activities include conditions such as drowsiness, lack of clarity in thought, maybe too much Guinness at the pub? These conditions surely could, and often do, lead to a belief's lacking warrant. Are these cases where my cognitive faculties are malfunctioning? Are they cases where I am mistaken or misjudge appearances?

It seems possible that while I am drowsy my cognitive faculties may function properly such that I have knowledge of basic things, such as that a is a. Yet on another level my faculties may be functioning incompletely such that I fail to have knowledge of ordinary things. For instance, because I am drowsy, and lack a certain critical reflection, I may make a mistake in my reasoning, similar to the way I may make an addition error in a math problem. Is Plantinga's view of proper function somehow supposed to protect against these sorts of instances, instances where I am mistaken because of drowsiness or negligence? Or does Plantinga want to guard against skeptical cases such as the Alpha Centurion cognitive scientist who is messing with my cognitive faculties such that my beliefs lack warrant? Does Plantinga want to account for both cases? I will expand on the notion of proper function and mistakes in judgment in chapter three. One thing is clear, Plantinga does not believe that proper function alone is sufficient for warrant. For he believes that one's cognitive faculties may be functioning perfectly, but in an environment not designed for those faculties so that one's beliefs may lack warrant.

Environment

To produce warrant, not only is proper function necessary, but so is an appropriate environment for our cognitive faculties. An appropriate environment for our cognitive faculties is just that environment for which they were intended or designed. Plantinga says that for warrant "your faculties must be in good working order, and the environment must be appropriate for your particular repertoire of epistemic powers."[17] Therefore, it is possible that the conditions on Alpha Centauri may be such that our cognitive faculties are not suited to the environment there and if by chance we found ourselves on Alpha Centauri our beliefs may lack warrant, though our faculties be functioning properly.

What is an appropriate environment for our cognitive faculties? How do we know whether we are in an appropriate environment? The notion of appropriate cognitive environment is a bit puzzling, yet it does seem as though we may have an idea of what may be considered inappropriate environments for clear thinking. A particularly noisy environment may not be conducive to clear thinking, and we are often quite aware of this. Take a noisy pub for example, a difficult place in which to think clearly indeed. Given that a certain graduate student may be indulging himself in one too many Guinness's in an inordinately noisy pub on a Friday night while trying to complete a logic proof for Monday's homework, it is reasonable to expect that he will not receive a very high grade on his homework come Monday. It is easy to see that this student's cognitive faculties may not be functioning altogether fully/critically in an appropriate environment. Yet this student could still have knowledge of some basic things even considering his functioning incompletely and in an inappropriate environment for clear, logical thinking. Even though this student may be inebriated, and his buddies singing at the top of their lungs, he may have knowledge of some things because at a fundamental level his cognitive faculties will never malfunction. This is so in any cognitive environment. I will argue this point further in a later chapter.

Design Plan

Plantinga says that there may be circumstances under which our faculties function properly and in an appropriate environment, but we may still lack warrant for our beliefs. For example, a woman who gave birth to a child years ago may now remember the pain of childbirth as much less than it actually was then. This belief, according to Plantinga, is one that lacks warrant. It lacks warrant because its aim is not truth but something else. Maybe this sort of belief is what allows for women to give birth more than once, for if they remembered the pain in its full intensity, they may never want to conceive again. As stated earlier, Plantinga claims, "human beings are constructed according to a certain design plan."[18] A design plan is "like a set of specifications for a well-formed, properly functioning human being."[19] These specifications include a plan for our cognitive faculties.

Plantinga gives special attention to the "importance of experience in the economy of our cognitive establishment."[20] He notes that there are different components to our cognitive makeup, each component having a different purpose or goal. But the relevant segment of the design plan for warrant is the portion that is aimed at truth. He says, "what confers warrant is one's cognitive faculties working properly, or working according to the design plan *insofar as that segment of the design plan is aimed at producing true beliefs.*"[21] Yet, one may have satisfied all of the above-mentioned conditions and *still* lack warrant. Why is that? Plantinga adds that the design plan must be a good one. He says:

> *The module of the design plan governing [a belief's]*

production must be such that it is objectively highly probable that a belief produced by cognitive faculties functioning properly according to that module (in a congenial environment) will be true or verisimilitudinous. This is the reliabilist constraint on warrant . . ..[22]

What exactly is this "reliabilist constraint?" I take it to mean that the module of the design plan that governs belief production is reliable, whether we are aware of it or not. The design plan, which is a good design plan, aimed at truth, allows for us to take for granted that our belief producing faculties are pretty reliable. If it is a good design plan under which we operate, there is no reason for us to doubt the reliability of our belief producing faculties.

Plantinga's alternative view of that quantity or quality enough of which makes true belief into knowledge is provocative and interesting. Yet, it is not without difficulties, some of which have already been mentioned. Some more basic, and thus more serious, objections to Plantinga's view of warrant will be examined in the following chapter.

[1]Plantinga, Alvin. *Warrant and Proper Function*. (New York: Oxford University Press, 1993), 4.
  [2]Ibid., 6.
  [3]Ibid.
  [4]Ibid.
  [5]Ibid., 7.
  [6]Ibid., 9.
  [7]Ibid., 13.
  [8]Ibid., 11.

[9] Ibid., 13.
[10] Ibid., 14.
[11] Ibid., 16.
[12] Ibid., 17.
[13] Ibid., 20.
[14] Ibid., 19.
[15] Ibid.
[16] Ibid., 6.
[17] Ibid., 7.
[18] Ibid., 13.
[19] Ibid., 14.
[20] Ibid., 16.
[21] Ibid.
[22] Ibid., 17.

3

Warrant Denied

Are the conditions of proper function, appropriate environment, and good design plan necessary and sufficient for warrant? Is warrant sufficient for knowledge? The best way to answer these questions is to examine Plantinga's epistemic system more critically. I will focus critical analysis on the notion of proper function. Why is it that Plantinga places the emphasis that he does on proper function, both in his rejection of classical internalism, and in his alternative view of warrant? If significant problems are apparent with this component of Plantinga's proposed view of warrant we may want to say that Plantinga's condition of proper function is not necessary for a theory of warrant, and furthermore, true belief plus Plantinga's alternative account of warrant (as proper function, appropriate environment, and good design plan) is not sufficient for knowledge.

Contra Proper Function

Plantinga rejects the traditional view of justification in favor of warrant, which he believes involves the proper function of our cognitive faculties. Concerning the proper function of our cognitive faculties Plantinga states, "let us provisionally entertain the idea that a belief has warrant for me only if the relevant parts of my noetic equipment - the parts involved in its formation and sustenance - are functioning properly."[1] Plantinga believes that our cognitive faculties may be unreliable. He claims that conditions such as "error, confusion and disagreement - show that our noetic faculties are to at least some degree unreliable."[2] Our noetic faculties would include the faculty of reason. Therefore, the cognitive faculty of reason may be unreliable.

If the faculty of reason is unreliable, and justification rests on reason/evidence, then it is possible that one be justified - that is have reasons for a belief, and not have knowledge. Is it the case that the faculty of reason is unreliable? Is there a difference between reason in itself (the laws of thought/logic) and a person's faculty of reason - a person's use of reason? I believe there is a difference and that Plantinga fails to emphasize the difference. Consequently, he blurs the distinction between reason in itself and a person's use of reason.

If the cognitive faculty of reason is reliable and wholly trustworthy, then it is possible to give reasons for belief such that these reasons guarantee the certainty of true belief similar to the way a sound argument guarantees the truth of an argument. I aim to show that Plantinga is unclear on either the subject of reason in itself or on a person's use of reason when he doubts the reliability of reason. Does he mean that the laws of thought/logic may be unreliable? Does he mean our use of reason (human faculty of reason) may malfunction and thus be unreliable? Is the possibility of cognitive malfunction, particularly that of reason, a factor which leads to his rejection of justification in favor of proper function and warrant? If it can be shown that reason does not malfunction, either in itself, or the faculty that we possess as rational beings, then it is possible that reason does get us to knowledge by means of justification in the traditional sense.

I would like to pause for a moment and define what I mean by reason and distinguish between reason in itself and our use of reason. Reason in itself I take to be the laws of thought. These include the law of identity (*a* is *a*); the law of non-contradiction (not both *a* and *non-a*); and the law of excluded middle (either *a* or *non-a*). Thinking – concept formation and making judgments – involves these laws. Reason in this sense, as the laws of thought, is infallible. As infallible, reason in itself is wholly trustworthy.

The laws of thought are not the whole story of logic. Rather, they are basic, possibly the most basic, laws of logic. Irving Copi, in his *Introduction to Logic*, says of these laws:

> *Those who have defined logic as a science of the laws of thought have often gone on to assert that there are exactly three fundamental or basic laws of thought necessary and sufficient for thinking to follow if it is to be "correct." These have traditionally been called "the principle of identity," "the principle of contradiction" (sometimes "the principle of noncontradiction"), and "the principle of excluded middle."*[3]

Copi's statement is important because it shows that there is a tradition that holds that reason is the laws of thought, and at least these three laws are basic to other logical principles. The laws of thought are the basic rules (not the only rules) by which we think and understand what is.

The laws of thought are natural laws of psychology that describe the way that our minds do in fact operate. They are not prescriptive laws; they are necessary laws. They are not cultural, nor are they conventional. The laws of thought are universal among rational beings. All rational beings use the law of identity, for example. Because the laws of thought are natural and universal laws, any being that thinks, does so according to these laws. For one to doubt this, one would have to use the laws of thought, i.e. we must make the judgment that we either think according to the laws of thought, or we do not think according to the laws of thought (*a* or *non-a*). Furthermore, since the laws of thought are not fallible, and are thus wholly trustworthy, the faculty of reason, which operates according to these laws is also reliable and wholly trustworthy.

It is difficult to ascertain from the literature what Plantinga's view of the nature of the laws of logic are, and whether our views are in accord. Yet, while speaking of *a priori* knowledge, of which the laws of thought are included, he speaks of seeing that "no dog is both an animal and nonanimal."[4] He then goes on to ask:

> ... *What does this 'seeing' consist in? It consists, first (I suggest), in your finding yourself utterly convinced that the proposition in question is* true. *It consists second, however, in finding yourself utterly convinced that this*

proposition is not only true, but could not have been false.[5]

Plantinga concludes this paragraph by stating, "reason is the faculty we learn of what is possible and necessary."[6] It is unclear from this passage alone whether Plantinga and I are in agreement about the status of the laws of thought, but judging from what he does say and his linking reason with necessary beliefs, he probably would not be in disagreement with the view of reason in itself that I have presented.

We should discuss two aspects of reason, reason as the laws of thought, and reason in its use (the faculty of reason). Within the use of reason, we can further distinguish between the descriptive and the normative use of reason. The descriptive is what we do (necessarily as thinkers). The normative is what we ought to do (and which implies moral obligation). The descriptive use of reason involves forming concepts, judgments, and arguments. It is used to interpret our experiences, and it is used to construct a coherent worldview. The descriptive use of reason is what all thinking beings in fact do with reason. Beyond the descriptive use of reason is the normative use of reason. The normative use of reason involves critically analyzing statements for meaning. Critical analysis as the normative sense of the use of reason has a moral imperative, we ought to use reason critically. Let us look at the uses of reason a bit more closely.

Concept formation is the first act of reason. When I form the concept "tree" I grasp the essence of tree, what is common to all trees and only trees, and I distinguish tree from all non-tree things (I distinguish *a* from *non-a*). In forming concepts and in distinguishing one thing from another, I am using reason.

Note that concept formation is not totally apart from sense perception. Most concepts are grasped through perception, although not all concepts are gotten in this way (*a priori*, for example).

Again, anytime we make a judgment we are using reason. A judgment involves two concepts joined by a copula (S is P). I would argue, furthermore, that anytime we have propositional knowledge a judgment is involved. When I know something, I at least know that S is P, as in the case when I know that the tree is green. Whether I come to believe that S is P through sense perception interpreted, or through testimony – Johnny tells me that S is P, or through memory – I remember that S is P, etc., reason is being used in forming the judgment S is P. In all these cases a judgment is made. Judgments are a form of the use of reason. Furthermore, arguments generally include two judgments (premises) and a conclusion. Therefore, reason is used to form arguments as well.

To understand how reason is used to interpret experience, I propose to examine what occurs in perception. In sense perception I am appeared to in a certain way. For instance, I look out the window and am appeared to greenly. I interpret this perception as "there is a tree outside." Sense perception gets us to appearances. These appearances then get interpreted through the use of reason as trees or cacti - the things that are perceived. When I go from being appeared to greenly to claiming, "the tree is green," I go from perception to making a judgment about that perception. "The tree is green" is a judgment of the form S is P. This judgment involves two concepts, "tree" and "green." Sense perception then is not a belief producing faculty in and of itself that may result in knowledge; sense perception brings information that gets interpreted by reason. Once interpreted, knowledge may (or may not) ensue.

Reason is used as a test for meaning; this is the critical, and normative, use of reason. We ought to use reason critically to analyze statements for meaning. If a statement lacks meaning, it cannot be true. For example, 'I have a square circle in my room' is a meaningless statement. It is logically impossible and therefore cannot be true. I know this by reason (I don't know it empirically). Reason is used as a test for meaning in that it is by reason that I am able to know that there are no square circles. There is no plane geometrical figure that exists in which all points are equidistant from the center and not equidistant from the center in the same respect and at the same time. Reason is the faculty that allows for me to analyze the meaning of terms. Reason is also used as a test for meaning in that we have to know what a statement means before we can judge whether it is true or not. For example, I cannot judge whether the statement 'bliks are grue' is true or not without understanding the meaning of the terms 'bliks' and 'grue'. If a statement lacks meaning, as 'bliks are grue' does for me, then I cannot judge whether it is true. Meaning is a necessary condition for truth, but it is not sufficient.

Lastly, reason may be used to construct a coherent world and life view. This is the constructive use of reason. All of the above mentioned uses of reason (with the possible exception of the use of reason as a test for meaning), fall under the descriptive sense of reason. This is the way rational beings operate, we form concepts, judgments and arguments; we interpret our experiences; we analyze the meaning of terms; we use reason constructively to build a worldview.

The normative sense of the use of reason is the critical

use of reason. We ought to use reason critically to be sure that the judgments we make are meaningful; we ought to be sure that the arguments we use are sound; we ought to be careful in interpreting our experiences, that we do not confuse appearance with reality; we ought to be sure the assumptions of our world view, upon which we build, are not faulty. We ought to use reason critically; this entails conscious and careful examination of concepts, judgments and arguments. Do we actually use reason in this way? We certainly can - there is no dysfunction that may keep me from using my (human faculty of) reason, but often times I do not use my (faculty of) reason critically. It seems as though if there is anything like cognitive malfunction it would be in this normative sense of the use of reason.

I would argue that reason in its use in the descriptive sense, does not malfunction. We do not fail to form concepts, judgments and arguments. We do not fail to interpret our experiences, and construct a world and life view. Yet we may fail to use reason critically (the normative sense) and make mistakes in our use of reason. If there is any sense of malfunction of our rational faculties, I believe this would be it. Yet, there is nothing that is broken or pathological in this sense of malfunction. I prefer to call this non-function because there is a lack of function in the critical use of reason. If mistakes arise in our beliefs, I would argue that reason has not been used fully/critically. For example, I may make a mistaken judgment, or I may have an argument that lacks soundness, this is not malfunction.

Often times we do not use reason critically though we may use it constructively to build a system of beliefs. When we use reason constructively without first using it critically to examine our assumptions for meaning, we may end up with a contradiction somewhere within our belief system. If this occurs, we ought to re-examine our beginning assumptions or premises for meaning to see if there are contradictory or incoherent beliefs.

Failure to use reason in one way may impact errors that come by means of using it another way. For instance, my failure to use reason critically may impact errors that occur when I use reason constructively. I may have a very coherent system of beliefs given my assumptions. Yet, because the beginning assumption was not critically examined for meaning, and it lacked meaning (i.e. it was incoherent) - it was mistaken. When I build a system of beliefs upon this faulty assumption, my whole system of beliefs may be wildly incorrect.

These are examples of the use of reason, and an explanation of how errors in our thinking may come about. I would like to use this distinction between reason in itself (the laws of thought) and reason in its use (both the descriptive and the normative senses) as a criticism of Plantinga's view of cognitive proper function. Plantinga seems to doubt the reliability of reason in some sense. Which sense of reason does Plantinga view as unreliable? May any of the forms of reason discussed above malfunction in any sense?

Plantinga defines cognitive malfunction as "the failure of the relevant cognitive faculties to function properly, to function as they ought to."[7] Cognitive malfunction may include a "damaging brain lesion, or the machinations of an Alpha Centurion scientist, or perhaps the mischievous schemes of a Cartesian evil demon."[8] Cognitive malfunction, according to Plantinga, may be due to pathologies;[9] high energy cosmic radiation;[10] being a brain-in-a-vat;[11] some Gettier circumstances;[12] and possibly being influenced by something like "black bile".[13] Cognitive malfunction may be due to something within a person such as a disease or delusion. Plantinga states that:

> *Like the rest of our organs and systems, our cognitive faculties can work well or badly; they can malfunction or function properly. They too work in a certain way to accomplish their purpose. The purpose of the heart is to pump blood; that of our cognitive faculties (overall) is to supply us with reliable information . . ..[14]*

Plantinga's view of malfunction throughout *WCD* and *WPF* is one of cognitive deception by outside influences such as Alpha Centurion cognitive scientists and evil demons, or internal influences such as damaging brain lesions and pathologies. He uses these examples of malfunction time and again to critique various views of justification.

An inference to be drawn concerning Plantinga's view of proper function as the way a thing ought to function is that if a thing does not do what it ought to do, if it malfunctions, it is not reliable and wholly trustworthy. Plantinga does not say as much, but if the proper function of the thermostat in my car is to regulate the temperature of my car and the thermostat malfunctions such that the car overheats, the thermostat is unreliable and renders the vehicle untrustworthy. If a bird's wing malfunctions it does not work as it ought to and it is not trustworthy. If our cognitive faculties could possibly malfunction, more particularly if reason may malfunction, could we not draw the same inference and claim it to be unreliable as well? If we may compare the proper function of our cognitive faculties to the proper function of other artifacts, and if malfunction of our cognitive faculties may similarly be compared to these artifacts, then it seems that the trustworthiness, or lack thereof, of our rational faculties may also be inferred.

How does Plantinga, given his theory of warrant, account for the ordinary case of a belief that lacks warrant? Is it a belief that is formed by one who is not being deceived by an outside influence, or inner disorder? Is cognitive malfunction, according to Plantinga, always involved in a belief's lacking warrant (assuming the belief is true, and I believe it in an appropriate environment according to a good design plan)? Is it possible for me to have knowledge even though I am under the influence of an evil demon, or have a brain tumor? Or are all beliefs unwarranted given these conditions? An outside influence or an inner disorder may affect our beliefs, yet is it ever the case that these influences or disorders may affect our ability to use reason at a basic level so as to allow for us to believe *a* is not *a*, that a thing is not what it is? Can reason at a fundamental level ever malfunction? I would argue that it cannot and it does not.

An Alpha Centurion cognitive scientist may be able to deceive my senses, and if Plantinga wants to call this malfunction it need not be disputed. What I am arguing is that this Alpha Centurion cognitive scientist (or a brain lesion) can never affect my cognitive faculties so as to lead me to believe what is logically impossible. He may affect my sensory beliefs, but he cannot affect logical truths that I have come to believe by means of reason. There are cases of brain damage that affect beliefs, which we may want to call malfunction, but we must state exactly what is malfunctioning in these cases. In such cases the brain itself is what is malfunctioning, not the individual's faculty of reason.

Cognitive error is not a matter of dysfunction or malfunction, but rather is due to something like lack of critical reflection, or non-function. When we make mistakes, we often say things like 'I just wasn't thinking when I did it,' or 'I should have known that, I wasn't thinking,' or 'I wasn't being careful.' Often times our minds are on cruise control, we go along without much critical reflection (reasoning) and we make mistakes because of negligence. If my mind wasn't engaged, or I was distracted, or something along these lines, is it a matter of malfunctioning or lack of function/ non-function? A lack of critical reflection is a shortcoming of sorts; it is a lack, not a malfunction. A shortcoming is the failure to do something that I should have, not a malfunction.

How would Plantinga's view need to be altered in order to take into account a view of non-function or a lack in critical reflection? It may be difficult, given Plantinga's externalist starting point, to account for the kind of critical reflection I suggest is necessary to avoid non-function. He may argue that we are not able to reflect critically before forming a belief. He may say that we just find ourselves with beliefs. Even if we were to grant that Plantinga's theory of warrant could account for the ability to critically reflect before assenting to belief, will he say that when I make a false judgment, because I was not critically reflecting, that this is cognitive malfunction? In this case, lack of critical reflection is my own fault (a neglect of duty), it is not due to an evil demon or random burst of high energy radiation. I was negligent. Negligence is a lack of something that ought to have been done, it is not "failure of the relevant cognitive faculties to function properly," unless we want to stipulate that proper function includes critical reflection upon forming and in maintaining what we have good reason to believe. It does seem that if Plantinga were to allow for an internalist view of critical reflection he may be able to say that lack of warrant in the case of the normal, healthy adult in an appropriate environment and operating according to a good design plan, is due to failure of critical reflection to function properly. He would have to add that it was not malfunction that led to the lack of warrant, but rather it was a case of non-function.

Given the distinction between cognitive malfunction and non-function, or lack of critical reflection, how does non-function explain counterexamples that are used to support malfunction? I will examine three such counterexamples. The first is the case where a student makes mistakes in his logic proofs. The second is the case where a person involved in an accident, and who has a brain injury, no longer believes that his leg is his own. Lastly, I will examine ordinary perceptual illusion using the case of the illusion of water on the highway.

How does Plantinga explain the case where a student repeatedly makes the same error in his logic proofs? Is it cognitive malfunction? If so, is it an outside influence or an inner disorder? I am not sure how Plantinga would answer. I would argue that the student that makes the same error in a logic proof has not understood the concepts involved. The student has not made the connections; he has not used reason fully. It may be asked, why has he not made the connections? Why has he not used reason fully? Is it because of malfunction? Arguing from experience, both as a student of logic and a professor of logic, I would say when a student makes mistakes in logic proofs that it is generally due to lack of attentiveness, lack of mental discipline, or it is due to negligence and poor study habits. Maybe the logic student really has a case of attention deficit disorder. Is ADD a case of cognitive malfunction? ADD seems to be a malfunction of the brain, but it may be corrected by the administration of appropriate drugs. A malfunction of the brain is not the same as a malfunction of reason. It may affect one's attention span and mental discipline, which in turn may limit how far one goes in the use of reason, but it is not a malfunction of reason.

I would like to address the example of the man involved in a serious skiing accident who, due to brain damage does not believe that his leg is his own.[15] Plantinga may classify this as a case of pathology, in which case, given his view, it would be a case of cognitive malfunction. In this example, one could reason with the man that this foot is attached to this leg, and this leg is attached to this body, this is your body, and since this leg is attached to your body, it is your leg. Apparently, the man could follow the argument quite well, but he would not accept the conclusion. I would have to say that there is malfunction of the brain in this case. And believing that there is a connection between mind and brain (a connection I do not think Plantinga would deny), it does seem that damage to the brain may affect the beliefs that one forms. In this case the man's brain damage affects the belief that he holds about his leg, namely that it is not his own. It does not seem to be a defect of reason - he is able to use reason to follow the argument about the foot being attached to the leg which is attached to his body. Yet he does not accept the conclusion that the leg is his own. I am unable to explain why he does not accept the conclusion (is anyone able to?) but I would venture to guess that it is attributable to his brain damage. I would agree with Plantinga that brain damage is a malfunction that affects beliefs.

Lastly, I will address the example of mistakes due to ordinary perceptual illusions, such as a belief formed that there is water on the highway on being appeared to that way, when in fact it is a visual illusion. Given a hot sunny day the highway often appears to have water on it though in fact there is no water (this phenomenon has to do with the radiation of heat). When we take the appearance of water to actually be water, what is going on? Is it a case of cognitive malfunction? I would argue that it is not cognitive malfunction (Plantinga may say that it is an issue of environment). I would say that it is a case of mistaken judgment.

A mistaken judgment occurs when I take the appearance of something to be reality. In this example I take the appearance of water on the highway to actually be water on the highway when in fact there is no water on the highway. These kinds of mistakes are understandable and occur quite frequently. They generally do not involve issues of great consequence, i.e. life or death, so we do not gather all the relevant information and supporting evidence before making the judgment that there is water on the highway. In cases of lesser consequence, less evidence is needed and mistakes may be made, but they are not usually grave mistakes. Perceptual errors do not seem to be malfunction, even given Plantinga's theory; they seem to be more issues of the environment.

One may ask at this point, why is it that lack of mental discipline, brain damage, and perceptual illusions are not cases of cognitive malfunction? If we want to call these things malfunction, I do not have to be in disagreement. I will raise the question of what exactly it is that is malfunctioning in these cases. These seem to be either cases of brain damage or cases where I have come short in the critical use of reason or in attentiveness. They are not the malfunction of reason. It is on the level of reason in itself and the descriptive sense of reason that malfunction does not occur. If we want to say that failure of the normative sense of the use of reason – failure to use reason critically – is a sort of malfunction, I will not object. Yet, in most cases of failure to use reason critically, we could have gone further but we came short and so ended up with an unwarranted belief, or even false belief. I prefer to call these failures cases of cognitive non-function to avoid confusion.

Plantinga and Reason

Throughout his trilogy concerning warrant, Plantinga discusses several views of rationality. To clarify what Plantinga means by reason, and whether he thinks this faculty may malfunction, I would like to examine four views of rationality that he presents and ask whether any of these senses of rationality may malfunction. The first sense of rationality that Plantinga discusses in *WCD* is what he terms "Aristotelian rationality." He states:

> *According to Aristotle, man is a rational animal. Aristotle was no doubt right in this as in much else: but what did he mean? One of the most venerable uses of the term 'rational' is to denote certain kinds of beings: those with* ratio, *the power of reason. Such creatures are able to hold beliefs; they are capable of thought, reflection, intentionality. Rational beings are those that are able to form concepts, grasp propositions, see relationships between them, think about objects both near and far.[16]*

Again, Plantinga says of Aristotelian rationality, in *Warranted*

Christian Belief (WCB), that:

> *The idea is that human beings, unlike at least some other animals, have concepts and can hold beliefs; they can reason, reflect, and think about things, even things far removed in space or time; human beings are (or at any rate, can be)* knowers. *This is what Aristotle saw as distinctive about human beings.*[17]

The Aristotelian sense of rationality is what I have been calling reason in its use in the descriptive sense, that is, reason is used to form concepts, judgments and arguments. I have attempted to argue that this sense of reason does not malfunction. We may infer from these two quotes that if Aristotle's sense of rationality is correct, then malfunction here may be malfunction of that which makes us human. I would argue that malfunction in this sense of reason would affect reason at such a fundamental level that we would not be able to form concepts, hold beliefs, and make judgments. In essence, we would not be able to think if this sense of reason were to malfunction. Furthermore, if thought is what makes humans rational, or different from non-rational beings, then malfunction of this sense of rationality would affect our humanity.

I could not find strong evidence that Plantinga believes that this sense of rationality may malfunction. Although in *WCB* he does say regarding irrationality that "irrationality . . . is a matter of malfunction of (some of) the rational faculties, the faculties by virtue of which we are rational animals."[18] I am not sure what to make of this quote, so I will give Plantinga the benefit of the doubt and continue with the view that the Aristotelian sense of rationality does not malfunction. The

Aristotelian sense of rationality roughly corresponds to what I have been calling reason in its use in the descriptive sense.

The second sense of rationality that Plantinga discusses in *WCD* is "rationality as the deliverances of reason." Plantinga says:

> *Aristotelian rationality is generic: it pertains to the power of thinking, believing and knowing. But there is also a very important more specific sense; this is the sense that goes with reason taken more narrowly, as the source of a* priori *knowledge and belief. Most prominent among the deliverances of reason are self-evident beliefs – beliefs so obvious that you can't grasp them without seeing that they couldn't be false.*[19]

This sense of reason would also fall under the category of reason that I have been calling the descriptive use of reason. Presumably, this sense of reason does not malfunction either, though Plantinga does not say as much. It is interesting to note that Plantinga says that "there are various analogical extensions of this use of the term 'rational' and its cohorts, and analogical extensions of the concept it expresses. First, we can broaden the category of reason to include memory and experience and whatever else goes into science."[20] It is in the area of memory and interpreting experience that I argue that we may fail to use reason critically and end up in error. Interestingly, Plantinga notes, directly after the quote above that "a person can be said to be irrational if he won't listen to or pay attention to the deliverance of reason."[21] Is this irrationality a case of malfunction or is it a case of negligence? It would seem that to avoid, resist, or deny reason is not malfunction in Plantinga's sense of external interference or internal pathology, but it is negligence or avoidance and is thus the non-use or non-function of one's rational faculties.

The third sense of rationality that Plantinga treats in *WCD* is what he calls "deontological rationality." He notes that rationality may have a deontological element to it and states that rationality "is very close to the classical notion of justification," and that "'justification' and 'rationality' are often used interchangeably (a fact we understand when we see that this variety of rationality, like classical justification, is essentially deontological."[22] This sense of rationality requires one to have rational justification or evidence for one's belief. Plantinga states that:

> *The term 'irrational' can come to be used as simply a name for a certain kind of behavior, a kind of behavior that, by many earlier users of the term, was thought to have the property (say, that of going contrary to duty) it expressed on the earlier use of the term. In this way someone can come to think that it is irrational to believe without propositional evidence . . ..[23]*

Since deontological rationality is closely connected to justification, and Plantinga is opposed to justification, it seems that he may look unfavorably upon this sense of rationality. He may want to say that deontological rationality falls prey to the same problems of malfunction (whatever they be) that deontological justification does. But this does not get us to exactly what that malfunction may be, which is the issue at hand.

Deontological rationality is similar to what I have been calling the use of reason in the normative sense - that we ought to use reason critically. Critical use of reason may include having reasons or evidence for what we believe. It also includes the duty to critically examine beliefs for meaning or rational coherence. I argue that we may come short or fail in this sense of the use of reason, but that this is not malfunction, rather it is a lack of function (non-function) at the critical level.

The fourth sense of rationality, and the final sense that I will discuss, is "rationality as sanity and proper function." Plantinga states that:

> *One who suffers from pathological confusion, or flight of ideas, or Korsakov's syndrome, or certain kinds of agnosia, or manic depressive psychosis will often be said to be irrational; after the episode passes, he may be said to have regained rationality. Here 'rationality' means absence of dysfunction, disorder, impairment, pathology with respect to rational faculties. So this variety of rationality is analogically related to Aristotelian rationality; a person is rational in this sense when no malfunction obstructs her use of the faculties by virtue of the possession of which she is rational in the Aristotelian sense.*[24]

What does Plantinga mean by irrationality and rationality here? Is malfunction of the rational faculties in this sense some sort of disorder in the brain or is there an obstruction of a person's use of reason in the descriptive sense? Is the pathological person still forming concepts, having beliefs, forming judgments, but they are just lacking in cogency? It seems as though rationality as sanity and proper function require a properly functioning brain for warrant to ensue. This seems true enough. Yet,

Plantinga wants to use this sense of irrationality and cognitive malfunction as an assault against justification. He argues against several views of justification based upon the fact that these views fail to account for proper function (of our rational faculties?). If by proper function Plantinga means everything is working right in my brain, then there will not be a whole lot of cases of cognitive malfunction. Most people have normally functioning brains. Plantinga's objections against justification are then based upon exceptions to the rule, rather than the normally functioning human being's lack of warrant. If this is what Plantinga means by cognitive malfunction, how will he account for the normal, healthy adult (not influenced by outside sources) in an appropriate environment and operating according to a good design plan who holds beliefs that clearly lack warrant? Must we stipulate that whenever a person's belief lacks warrant it must either be malfunction or something wrong with the environment or design plan rather than the person's not having gone far enough in the use of reason?

I agree with Plantinga that there are cases of brain damage, and that this is a malfunction. But it seems that even if a person has brain damage of some sort, or is pathological or depressed, that person may still hold beliefs and have knowledge of some basic things. The pathological person sill has properly functioning rational faculties in that he cannot believe both *a* and *not a* in the same respect and at the same time. He cannot believe that he both sees a tree before him and does not see a tree before him. He cannot believe that someone both is and is not out to get him. If he has this basic function of reason intact he can hold many true beliefs and know many things and all the while be a pathological nut. I can be a pathological maniac and still know by reason that being cannot arise from absolute non-being. I can know that there are no square circles. If I can know these things, I can use reason to build upon these basic pieces of knowledge.

Cases of brain damage, pathology, outside influences etc., may be cases of malfunction of the brain. But malfunction in this sense is rare and is the exception to the rule and should not determine the rule. The rule is the ordinary, healthy adult who can (and should) use reason critically to examine assumptions but does not. This happens far more often than the brain damaged, shouldn't the normal then be our focus? The case of the normal adult that lacks warrant is the more philosophically interesting case.

At this point it may be worthwhile to note that Plantinga, in developing his design plan in *Warrant and Proper Function*, seems to derive most of his "properly basic beliefs" from Thomas Reid's "first principles." Would Plantinga depart from Reid on the issue of the trustworthiness of the faculty of reason? Reid's seventh of the "first principles" states that:

> *The natural faculties by which we distinguish truth from error, are not fallacious. If any man should demand a proof of this, it is impossible to satisfy him. For, suppose it should be mathematically demonstrated, this would signify nothing in this case; because to judge of a demonstration, a man must trust his faculties, and take for granted the very thing in question.*[25]

Again Reid states:

> *If any truth can be said to be prior to all others in the order of nature, this seems to have the best claim; because,*

> *in every instance of assent, whether upon intuitive, demonstrative, or probable evidence, the truth of our faculties is taken for granted, and is, as it were, one of the premises on which our assent is grounded.[26]*

Lastly, it is interesting to note what Keith Lehrer, a contemporary and peer to Plantinga says concerning this point. Lehrer states that both he and Plantinga:

> *. . . Are admirers of the writings of Thomas Reid and appeal to his writings and ideas in defense of our own. Plantinga is, in some ways, closer to Reid in the central role that he gives to the functioning of our faculties, but I attach greater importance than Plantinga does to a central principle of Reid's, the seventh of Reid's first principles concerning contingent truths, which affirms that "our natural faculties by which we distinguish truth from error are not fallacious" and are worthy of our trust. Reid says that our assent to all the other principles is grounded upon this one. . . .This seventh principle is a kind of metaprinciple because it vouches for the convictions resulting from our faculties and thus offers internal evidence for them, as it also vouches for itself and offers internal evidence for itself.[27]*

Reid and Lehrer both seem to hold to the conviction that our cognitive faculties by which we distinguish truth from error, (I take this to at least include the faculty of reason) are not fallacious. While Reid and Lehrer may hold that the faculty of reason is not fallacious, it is unclear as to whether Plantinga is in agreement, as we shall further investigate.

Reid seems to think that the deliverances of reason and the deliverances of the senses are on a par, for he says, "the faculties of consciousness, of memory, of external sense, and of reason, are all equally the gifts of nature. No good reason can be assigned for receiving the testimony of one of them, which is not of equal force with regard to the others." [28] The deliverances of reason and the senses are both first-principles, or self-evident, and both are trustworthy, according to Reid. He says:

> *If our faculties be fallacious, why may they not deceive us in this reasoning as well as in others? . . . Every kind of reasoning for the veracity of our faculties, amounts to no more than taking their own testimony for their veracity . . . .[29]*

It is unclear as to whether Plantinga follows Reid in the belief about the trustworthiness of reason. He states, "often we *do* believe the faculty of reason more than that of perception, and rightly so."[30]

He then asks:

> *What about reason itself? Is there something about it that distinguishes it from other faculties, such that by virtue of that feature it is more worthy of credence than the others? I am inclined to think the answer is yes, although I am unable, at present, to see the issues with real clarity.[31]*

This is a very important point to note. I believe that it is Plantinga's lack of a strong view, and clarity on the issue of reason that may lead to his development of the alternative view of warrant. Is the faculty of reason unreliable? Is it fallacious? Can the faculty of reason be trusted? If the faculty of reason is unreliable and cannot wholly be trusted then the development of a theory of warrant based upon the proper function of our cognitive faculties to guarantee truth, because reason may not be able to do so, seems like a logical step to make. Plantinga need not depart from Reid and Lehrer. Why not develop a stronger sense of the role of reason and its relation to cognitive proper function? If Plantinga were to do so, would he need to reject justification altogether?

An Alternative view of Reason

I argue that reason in itself, as the laws of thought, is wholly trustworthy. The laws of thought are basic laws that govern our very thought process. It is not conceivable that these laws be fallible. It is logically impossible that *a* is both *a* and *non-a* in the same respect and at the same time. It is logically impossible that any sentence in this paper be both true and false in the same respect and at the same time. This is true of all logically possible worlds. In this sense reason in itself is infallible and absolutely reliable.

It is possible to misuse reason or not use reason fully such that we end up in error or false belief. Plantinga argues that since we sometimes end up with contradictory conclusions that we cannot possibly accept, we may question the reliability of reason. He asks could not "someone who had encountered a deliverance of reason that by apparently self-evident argument forms led to an apparently self-evidently false conclusion . . . stop trusting reason? I can't see why not."[32] But it seems obvious by the very fact that we cannot possibly accept contradictory conclusions that reason in itself is alive and well and *very* trustworthy for it is only by reason that we are able to recognize contradictions. If we could possibly begin to believe explicit contradictions, then we would be in dire straits and ought to be in intellectual despair. Reason in itself dictates that it is always impossible for self-contradictory statements to be true in the same respect at the same time. One may fail to use reason in argumentation such that he ends up with a contradictory conclusion, but if this occurs, then the problem must have been in one's use of reason and not in the laws of thought. If we end up with a contradiction, we have failed to use reason critically; we have failed in the normative sense of reason.

What does Plantinga say about the faculty of reason? He says:

> *An important difference between reason and my other faculties is the obvious fact that I can't think about the reliability of any of my faculties without in some sense trusting reason, taking it for granted or assuming, at least for the time being, that it is reliable.[33]*

He then goes on to ask whether there is a relevant difference between trusting perception and trusting reason. He thinks there is a difference and states:

> *Is it a relevant difference? I think it is, but it is hard to explain exactly why. Perhaps the answer lies in the following slightly different direction: we cannot so much as raise the question of the reliability of reason, or any other of our faculties, without taking the reliability of*

> *reason for granted.[34]*

Plantinga concludes that there is a relevant difference between the trustworthiness of our senses and of reason, which seems correct. Yet, he asks the question, "What would be required for me to conclude, sensibly, that reason is not to be trusted?"[35] Why would he ask this question when he has already taken the trustworthiness of reason for granted? When Plantinga asks this question about the trustworthiness of reason what does he have in mind? Is he questioning the trustworthiness of the faculty of reason in the descriptive sense? Is he questioning the trustworthiness of the faculty of reason in the normative sense, the critical use of reason? This seems unclear, and Plantinga's motivation for asking the question seems equally unclear. He tries to show that the "human faculty" of reason may not be trustworthy by arguing the following:

> *What is needed . . . is a case where reason somehow indicts itself, and cannot self-servingly point the finger at something else, some other faculty. Suppose there were some propositions that are among the immediate teachings of reason – that is, were apparently self-evident; and suppose they led by argument forms also sanctioned by reason to a conclusion whose denial was an immediate teaching of reason. To put it more simply, suppose I came upon apparently self-evident propositions P1 . . ., Pη that led by apparently self-evidently valid arguments to a self-evidently false conclusion Q. If reason is reliable, then P1 . . ., Pη are true; but if P1 . . ., Pη are true, then so is Q, in which case reason is not reliable; so if reason is reliable, it isn't reliable; so it's not reliable. Could I sensibly come*

to this conclusion and no longer trust reason?[36]

He seems to suggest that if this were to occur, we would be stuck in a circle of trusting reason, and using reason to mistrust reason, and ultimately mistrusting reason altogether and then returning to naturally trusting reason again "until I am in effect intellectually paralyzed."[37]

My response to Plantinga is that I would like to see a real example where logically self-evident propositions, lead by logically self-evidently valid arguments to a logically self-evidently false conclusion, so as to indict reason itself. I do not mean *apparently* self-evident propositions and *apparently* self-evidently valid arguments leading to an *apparently* false conclusion. The contradiction that Russell found in Frege's proof was of this kind. It had an apparently self-evident premise that lead to a contradiction in the conclusion. Once Frege recognized that there was a contradiction he had to give up the premise. I do not believe that Plantinga, or anyone else, could come up with an actual example where logically self-evident propositions, led by logically self-evidently valid arguments to a logically self-evidently false conclusion. This, I would add, is logically impossible. The very fact that I know this is proof that reason is most trustworthy. It cannot be reason in itself that Plantinga doubts as trustworthy. Couldn't it be that he wants to doubt the reliability of our use of reason?

Question: Has the person in Plantinga's above example, who came to the contradictory conclusion, used reason critically in reaching his conclusion? If he can recognize that there is a contradiction in the conclusion of the argument has he not used reason to see the contradiction? In this sense his cognitive faculty of reason is functioning quite well. Should he maybe go back and re-examine his premises to see if there is an error before rejecting the reliability of reason itself or the faculty of reason? After all, Plantinga did say that they were *apparently* self-evident propositions.

What is meant by "apparently self-evident" here? Does Plantinga distinguish between what is psychologically self-evident, such as in the way I am appeared to, and what is logically self-evident, as in the law of non-contradiction? Psychological self-evidence is the way it seems to me, whereas logical self-evidence is what cannot be otherwise - it is the way things actually *are*. I may be mistaken in the judgment about what is psychologically self-evident, but I cannot be mistaken in the logically self-evident. If the logically self-evident can be mistaken sometimes it may be mistaken anytime. The logically self-evident includes the laws of thought/logic. If the laws of thought/logic cannot be trusted at one point, they cannot be trusted at any point. There would be no way to verify whether reason in the sense of the laws of thought/logic is mistaken. How would we know that we are mistaken in the logically self-evident? We would have no way to verify that we are mistaken. If we are mistaken in the psychologically self-evident, we may be able to verify that what we have mistakenly taken to be self-evident is not actually self-evident by means of reason. In the case of the logically self-evident we cannot conceive of the opposite being true without it entailing a contradiction. For example, the psychologically self-evident for me right now is that there appears to be a computer before me. The opposite of this may be false. Conceiving that there really is no computer before me, though there appears to be one does not involve contradiction. But if I claim that there is a computer and there is not a computer before me there is a contradiction. Both claims necessarily cannot be true in the same respect and at the same time.

Maybe after reflection the apparently self-evident propositions that Plantinga speaks about will not actually be self-evident, as in Frege's case. Maybe they are psychologically self-evident, and subject to mistake, but not logically self-evident. It seems as though if a person should have a conclusion similar to the one Plantinga offers something has gone wrong in the argument process, in the *use* of reason (in the normative sense), not in reason itself. For we are still able to see, through reason itself, the contradiction in the conclusion. The fact that we know there is a contradiction is proof that the faculty of reason has not been used fully or has been misused in the formulation of the original argument.

The objection may come that Plantinga is talking about certain circumstances where reason may not be trustworthy, such as in set theoretic and semantic paradoxes. Thus, one may say, reason is unreliable in a very restricted sense. Set theoretic and semantic paradoxes fall under a narrow sub-set of reason, if reason may be unreliable here, what keeps it from being unreliable everywhere else? If reason may be fallacious in a narrow sub-set of reason, then why may it not be fallacious in a more broad and general sense of reason as well? Again, it seems that if reason can be unreliable somewhere, then it can be unreliable everywhere.

Even if I were to conclude that Plantinga does not explicitly state that reason is unreliable, that he tries to argue for the reliability of reason, even if he were to state that reason is wholly trustworthy, his very theory of proper function undermines the claim. For a theory of proper function assumes that our cognitive faculties (reason included) may (and do) in fact malfunction. And if they may (and do), then they are not wholly reliable.

Yet, if the faculty of reason is reliable, not fallacious, and is therefore trustworthy, proper function is a given and Plantinga's theory of warrant is not necessary. If reason is trustworthy, justification – having reasons for belief, in conjunction with true belief may get us to knowledge. It must be noted that this is only possible if a person uses reason fully and critically and does not misuse reason. Furthermore, if reason is wholly trustworthy, it would be so in any cognitive environment. It would be trustworthy on Alpha Centauri, in all possible worlds, in South Bend, Indiana, etc.

Proper function is guaranteed if reason is trustworthy, and Plantinga need not come up with an elaborate view to supplement the reliability of reason. Secondly, if reason is reliable, it may lead us to knowledge. We may want to suggest that it is the full and unadulterated use of reason that is necessary and sufficient for warrant, or what I prefer to call justification.

One may say that this objection to warrant is too narrowly focused upon reason and that surely Plantinga believes that there are other cognitive faculties besides reason. It is true that Plantinga thinks that our "cognitive establishment" includes other faculties such as perception, testimony, memory beliefs, and many others. I will examine this objection by taking a closer look at what Plantinga says about our other cognitive faculties.

Before moving on to the other cognitive faculties that we possess, I would like to suggest that though there may be other faculties in our cognitive establishment, there is one primary knowledge-producing faculty. My objection to Plantinga's view of proper function thus far has been focused upon his view of the cognitive faculty of reason, and whether reason, in any sense, may malfunction. I have focused on reason because if we have knowledge, it is through the faculty of reason that we know. If S knows that P, then S believes that P. If S believes that P, then S thinks that P. If S thinks that P, then S has the concept P. If S has the concept P, S has formed the concept P by means of reason. Therefore, if S knows that P, S knows that P by means of reason.

I want to argue that reason is our primary knowledge-producing faculty. I say 'primary,' because the senses do play an initial and important role in most of our concept formation. Since reason does not malfunction, and it is our primary knowledge-producing faculty, we always have the ability to know.

Cognitive Faculty of Sense Perception

Plantinga states, in detailing his design plan, that our cognitive faculties:

> *. . . Produce beliefs on an enormously wide variety of topics – our everyday external environment, the thoughts of others, our own internal lives. . ., the past, mathematics and logic, what is probable and improbable, what is necessary and possible, beauty, right and wrong, our relationships to God, and a host of other topics.[38]*

He then goes on to list what I take to be our cognitive faculties when he says:

> *. . . We believe on the basis of sense experience, testimony,*

memory, mathematical and logical intuition, philosophical intuition, introspection, extrospection (whereby we come to know the thoughts and feelings of others), induction, evidence from other beliefs, and (so I say, anyway) Calvin's sensus divinitatis.[39]

Six chapters of *WPF* are dedicated to "a whirlwind tour of some of the main modules of our epistemic establishment: self-knowledge, memory, perception, knowledge of other persons, testimony, *a priori* knowledge, induction, and probability."[40] Plantinga seems to believe that these various cognitive faculties, or "modules of our epistemic establishment," are belief-producing mechanisms. Are these faculties on an equal par with regard to belief production or formation? Are they all liable to malfunction?

An Alternative View of The Senses

I have attempted to argue that the cognitive faculty of reason cannot fail to function properly. What do we say about the other cognitive faculties that we possess, particularly that of sense perception? May these other cognitive faculties malfunction? I would like to argue that the other cognitive faculties that we possess do not malfunction. I would like to specifically address the faculty of sense perception. As it is not the faculty of reason that does not malfunction, but rather it is a person's application of reason, our failure to use reason, that may be mistaken, so I want to argue that the faculty of sense perception in itself does not malfunction, but it is our interpretation of what is perceived (interpretation through lack of the critical use of reason) that may be mistaken. I would like to argue, further, that there is a difference between a mistaken judgment (a failure in the use of reason), and cognitive malfunction.

Plantinga states at the beginning of *WPF* that the "notion of proper function is the rock on which the canvassed accounts of warrant founder."[41] He reminds us of the example of "Chisholm's dutiful epistemic agent who, whenever he is appeared to redly, always believes that nothing is appearing redly to him," he adds that:

> *Chisholm's agent meets Chisholm's conditions for warrant; his beliefs lack warrant, however, because they result from cognitive dysfunction due to a damaging brain lesion, or the machinations of an Alpha Centurion scientist, or perhaps the mischievous schemes of a Cartesian evil demon.[42]*

Does this cognitive agent have any control over his believings? Is he able to critically reflect upon what he finds himself believing? It seems that mistakes in our judgment come in when we "find ourselves" believing without critical reflection concerning whether what appears to us is in fact reality. It is not always the case that appearance and reality coincide. Our faculties of sense perception function quite properly in giving us appearances. Yet, once I make a judgment about those appearances, I am liable to err.

Is the failure to yield correct judgment a case of cognitive malfunction, according to Plantinga's view? If mistaken judgment is what Plantinga means by cognitive malfunction, then whenever I am mistaken in my judgments, it may be attributed to something going wrong with my faculties, not with my judgment itself. If this is what Plantinga means by malfunction, then how can we hold persons accountable for their actions? I could not say to the police officer who pulls me over for speeding, "I am sorry officer, I misjudged the speed of my vehicle. You know how it is, cognitive malfunction." This cannot be what Plantinga means by cognitive malfunction, for I could make a mistake in judgment and then correct the judgment. When I do this several times a day is this malfunction and then proper function in quick succession? Plantinga must mean something else besides a cognitive faculty is malfunctioning if it does not yield correct judgments. In what sense, then, may we speak of the proper function of the cognitive faculty of sense perception?

Plantinga says "cognitive malfunction [is] failure of the relevant cognitive faculties to function properly, to function as they ought to." [43] Is it ever the case that our faculties do not function "as they ought to?" Does he mean that we may fail to use reason critically? We have seen that cognitive malfunction is not the same as the failure to yield correct judgment. What then does Plantinga mean by cognitive malfunction? Maybe if we look at some ordinary examples of perception, and perceptual error, we may be able to see that what Plantinga may want to attribute to cognitive malfunction is not malfunction at all, but rather mistaken judgment, a mistake in the normative use of reason.

Let us use an actual example to illustrate the point concerning mistaken judgment verses cognitive malfunction. I park my car in an unusually large parking lot at school, I know the aisle in which I parked my car. After class I go to the parking lot, to the aisle that I parked my car, and go to a green car, that appears to be my green car, parked in the aisle that I parked my car. I believe this green car, that appears to be my green car, is my car, after all I did leave it in this aisle. Upon further inspection (the key does not unlock the door), I find that it is not my car but is exactly like my car. My car is actually one car over, hidden behind a large sport utility truck. If I had looked at the license plate, I would have noticed this was not my car. In making the mistaken judgment that the green car in the parking lot was mine, when it actually was not, is there some malfunctioning going on? Is there some kind of cognitive dysfunction, or was I just forming a belief based on insufficient evidence and lack of attentiveness?

It does not seem as though cases of mistaken judgments are due to cognitive malfunction. My senses were working properly in yielding the appearance of what seemed to be my car, it was the exact make, model, and color, nothing was malfunctioning here. Yet, when I made the judgment that this green car is my green car, I was just mistaken. My cognitive faculty of sense perception was working perfectly, but I still made a mistake. The mistake was due to my making a judgment based on insufficient information; it was due to a lack of attentiveness.

The senses give me appearances. The faculty may work poorly or well in giving these appearances for example, I may need to wear glasses to see clearly. However, when I make a judgment about these appearances, I may make a mistake. Appearance is not reality, and when I take the appearances to be reality is when I may make a mistaken judgment. For example, I may see a person on campus that I take to be my friend Mary. My senses work perfectly in delivering this appearance to me (to be sure, I am wearing my glasses). Yet, when I make the judgment that this is my friend Mary, when it is actually my friend's twin sister Suzy, then I am mistaken in my judgment. I am mistaken because I took the appearance of my friend Mary to be the reality of my friend. There is no cognitive malfunction involved here. Perhaps I say, "Hello Mary," to the person I take to be my friend, and she says, "I am Suzy, not Mary. Mary is in Chemistry class." I would then correct my mistaken judgment that this is my friend, rather, given this new evidence, I would reform my belief to 'this is my friend's twin.'

Maybe this is an alien posing as the twin of my friend Mary, and I am still mistaken in my judgment about the identity of this being who has the appearance of my friend Mary. I may have a mistaken judgment that clearly lacks warrant, but not because of cognitive malfunction. Rather, I am mistaken because appearance and reality are not in accord and I make a judgment based on the (uncritical) assumption that they are in accord and I am mistaken in my judgment. Mistaken judgments are due, not to malfunction, but to insufficient evidence or information. It is difficult to see how the term 'malfunction' may be applied to our cognitive faculties.

Do I have any control over my believings? If for some reason I just "find myself believing" that I am appeared to orangely upon hearing a church bell, I need not form the belief that the orange that I perceive is real. The sound of church bells and the appearance of orange is not something that my cognitive establishment has encountered in the past. I may ask someone nearby, "Are you perceiving 'orange' right now? Is that church bell sound producing the appearance of orange to you?" If they say "No, are you crazy?" Then I may say to myself, I am appeared to orange, but the orange may not be real. Maybe those evil demons are playing me tricks again. I think I shall withhold the belief that there is something orange when I am appeared to orange upon hearing the church bell. I will need more evidence before forming this belief, currently it lacks warrant for me.

A more realistic example may be that I am sitting in my cottage and I am appeared to aurally in the raining outside sort of way. Rather than forming the belief that it is raining outside, when I am appeared to in that way, I think for a minute - there are no clouds outside, it has not rained in 110+ days, rain is not in the forecast. It must be something other than rain that I am hearing. I will further investigate. I go outside to find that there is absolutely no rain. If I had formed the belief that it is raining outside upon being appeared to in that fashion I would have been mistaken. Since I did not make the judgment that it is raining, but sought to gather further information, I was able to avoid error. I withheld the belief that it is raining outside. I do not know the source of the appearance of the sound of rain, but I did have control over whether I believed that it was raining or not. I decided not to believe based upon the overwhelming evidence to the contrary.

Currently, I may form the belief that I am in a room at school writing a paper. I form this belief based upon many different things. All my senses are active in forming this belief. I hear the activity of other students; I taste and smell the coffee I am drinking; I see the paper on the table before me; I feel the pencil in my hand. There is something that assimilates and interprets all of these sensations together to form the belief that I am in a room at school writing a paper. It is the interpretive use of reason. The interpretive use of reason, when not used critically, may result in misinterpretation, mistaken judgment, error, etc. Is misinterpretation the same as malfunction?

Cognitive Mistake, Not Malfunction

Ronald Beanblossom, in the introduction to Thomas Reid's, *Inquiry and Essays*, states that "the agent cannot be mistaken as to what sensations or appearances he is having, but he can misinterpret those sensations."[44] He goes on to quote Reid as saying:

> *'The appearances of things to the eye always corresponds to the fixed laws of Nature; therefore, if we speak properly, there is no fallacy in the senses . . . . but we sometimes mistake the meaning of the signs, either through ignorance of the laws of Nature, or through ignorance of the circumstances which attend the signs.'[45]*

The same cognitive faculty may be involved in yielding both true and mistaken judgments. This is not due to the faculty itself not functioning properly, but rather it is due to a misapplication of the faculty, or a misinterpretation of the information gotten from the senses. Perceptual error seems to be due not to the malfunction of my perceptors, but to the misinterpretation, or misjudgment, of my perceptions. The senses do not malfunction in giving us appearances; we cannot be mistaken about how we are appeared to. Yet, when we claim that what is appearing to me is reality, when I make judgments about appearances, and in fact I am wrong, I have misjudged and am mistaken. When I claim that I see my friend, I am appeared to in the friend sort of way, but it is not my friend but my friend's twin, I am mistaken in my judgment of reality, though my sense perception was correct in giving me the appearance of my friend. This is an understandable case of misjudgment, but it is not malfunction.

What about cases of cognitive deception? Are these cases of malfunction? It seems as though if I am deceived by a Cartesian demon, or Alpha Centurion cognitive scientist, to believe that I perceive something that is orange, when in fact there is no orange thing, the demon or scientist must somehow bypass my ordinary way of perception and impress my mind directly with this perceptual belief. It seems that the neural impulses in my brain still produce the mental image of something that is orange, and this is how the ordinary perceptual process usually goes, only the image would come through the faculty of sight first. In the case of cognitive deception, I do not notice that the ordinary perceptual process has been interfered with. Though the perceptual input process has been tampered with in the case of deception, we still have proper function in believing we are appeared to in a certain way. I may still believe that I am appeared to in a way that something is orange, but if I make the claim that there actually is something that is orange, when in fact there is not, I am mistaken, though understandably so.

It seems as though we may apply this account of mistaken judgment, verses cognitive malfunction, to all of our other cognitive faculties as well. For example, let us briefly examine memory beliefs. If I remember that I had eggs for breakfast this morning, but in fact I did not have eggs for breakfast, I had pancakes, then I am mistaken in my memory belief. Yet, I function quite properly in remembering it seems to me that I had eggs for breakfast this morning. I cannot be mistaken about what seems to be, but when I make the judgment that I had eggs for breakfast when in fact I did not, then I am mistaken, I am misremembering. The same cognitive faculties that are involved in actually remembering are involved with misremembering as well, and these faculties are functioning quite well. I have made a mistake that is due to a judgment about the content of the memory, rather than to the faculty of memory itself. Misremembering is often a case of misjudgment of an occurrence of the past. The faculty of memory is not dysfunctional.

We may want to ask whether Gettier cases are examples of cognitive malfunction or are they cases of judgments based upon insufficient evidence and therefore mistaken judgments? Misjudgment is not knowledge, but it is not malfunction either. Misjudgment is a mistake in reasoning. Misjudgments are due to uncritically held assumptions. For example, I may uncritically take the appearance of two sheep in the field to be two sheep in the field when in actuality there is a sheep and a sheep-shaped rock in the field. I uncritically take appearance to be reality in this case. This is an understandable mistake, and if my life depended upon this judgment, I may be more careful than taking appearance to be reality, I would try to obtain further evidence before making the judgment. Maybe I would walk into the field and touch the sheep. This is not a case of malfunction but rather it is a case of the failure to use reason critically.

Plantinga's notion of cognitive malfunction is at best unclear. It is difficult to see exactly what he may mean by cognitive malfunction. Many of the examples that he uses to show malfunction may be explained otherwise, such as not using reason fully, misjudging appearances, or making judgments based upon insufficient information or lack of evidence. If Plantinga wants to call these instances of "malfunction," fine, but how will his theory of warrant account for them? Apparently, these sorts of errors, or malfunctioning, will still occur given his theory of warrant.

In conclusion, proper function of our cognitive faculties is something that we always have. Consequently, Plantinga's account of proper function is not necessary for warrant. If we always have proper function, we may want to keep the traditional view of justification, which Plantinga views as seriously lacking as an account of knowledge because of its failure to account for proper function. Since I always have proper function, and error in my judgments about appearances may be avoided by critical reflection (I am able to critically reflect because reason is trustworthy), and having sufficient evidence for belief, it may be a duty for me to make judgments only upon having sufficient reasons or evidence. A quote from Keith Lehrer in his essay, *"A Critique of Externalism,"* sums up this notion nicely. He says:

> *The reliability essential to justification is not the reliability of the process which produces or causally sustains belief. What is essential is the reliability or trustworthiness of the evidence for what we accept to guide us to acceptance of what is true rather than false. The trustworthiness of the evidence makes us trustworthy in the matter, whatever our general defects. In epistemology as in life generally, you do not have to be perfect in order to be justified.[46]*

Having appropriate reasons, or evidence, for a belief is still necessary (and nearly sufficient) for warrant, or what I prefer to call justification.

Conclusion and Implications for Knowledge

The traditional view of knowledge is that knowledge is justified true belief. Justification involves having appropriate reasons for true belief. Appropriate reasons are what comes from my faculty of reason applying the laws of thought (logic) in a way such that proof of the objective truth of the belief is the result. Having reasons includes both the descriptive and the normative senses of reason. Having reasons entails judgments and arguments, which is the descriptive sense of reason, and the fact that we ought to critically reflect in the process of having such reasons involves the normative sense of reason.

If either reason itself (the laws of thought/logic), or the cognitive faculty of reason (in either the descriptive or the normative senses) may be unreliable, then reasons for true belief may not be sufficient, along with true belief, for justification. If reason itself (the laws of thought/logic) is fallible, we may not be able to know what argument forms are reliable so as to aid in providing appropriate reasons for true belief. We could not know whether an argument was sound if reason itself was fallacious.

If my cognitive faculty of reason (the use of reason in the descriptive sense) may be unreliable, then perhaps we may lack the ability to form concepts, judgments and arguments in pursuit of appropriate reasons for belief. If the human faculty of reason is unreliable then I may have an unreliable faculty that could lead me to doubt whether any of my knowledge claims are justified, for, how would I know whether I believe upon having appropriate reasons. We would not have certainty regarding how our faculties do function.

Plantinga calls into doubt, either explicitly, or by his theory of malfunctioning cognitive faculties, the absolute trustworthiness of either one or the other of these two senses of reason. It is unclear, given Plantinga's view, whether reason itself or the human faculty of reason are wholly trustworthy and fully reliable.

To doubt reason itself (the laws of thought/logic), or the cognitive faculty of reason (our use of reason), is to doubt whether we can derive appropriate reasons for true belief. For, either the laws of logic, or my application of those laws may be unreliable, and so unable to produce appropriate reasons for true belief.

If justification involves having appropriate reasons - either by the laws of logic, or by my using the laws to come up with an argument, and the laws or the means by which I come up with appropriate reasons are flawed, then justification, along with true belief, would not be sufficient for knowledge.

It is not the case that either the laws of logic, or my cognitive faculty of reason is unreliable - both are wholly trustworthy. To question either the laws of logic or my faculty of reason would require for me to both acknowledge the laws of logic as valid (I would have to use an argument, which assumes the trustworthiness of logic) and my ability to apply those laws as trustworthy in forming an argument against reason. To question reason (either in itself, or my faculty) would require me to assume the trustworthiness of reason in the very process of questioning reason.

I would conclude that justification - that is, having appropriate reasons, plus true belief - is sufficient (possibly with the addition of some fourth condition) for knowledge. If justification along with true belief is sufficient, we do not need Plantinga's theory of warrant to supplement (or supplant) the traditional view of justification.

Proper function is what is most significant to Plantinga's theory of knowledge. Appropriate environment and the design plan are important for Plantinga's theory in that they help to support and explain proper function. Knowledge, in Plantinga's view, is true belief produced by cognitive faculties that function properly in an appropriate environment, according to a good design plan. While I believe that there are questions to be raised regarding the other two components of Plantinga's theory of Warrant (environment and design plan), I have focused my criticism on his view of Proper function of our cognitive faculties. According to Plantinga, proper function, appropriate environment and good design plan are each necessary conditions for warrant, and together are sufficient for warrant.

I have attempted to show that proper function, as one of the conditions for knowledge, is not a necessary condition for an account of warrant. I argue that we always have proper function of our cognitive faculties. Our faculties are trustworthy and reliable. Giving a theory of proper function or proposing it as a condition for knowledge is not necessary.

Plantinga rejects the traditional view of justification (knowledge is justified true belief) because theories of justification fail to account for the possibility of cognitive malfunction. What I argue is that if we do not have cognitive malfunction, theories of justification do not have to consider the possibility of cognitive malfunction (they may have to consider the possibility of non-function, i.e. lack of critical reflection). If Plantinga's objection to justification is on the basis of malfunction, and there is no malfunction, then Plantinga's objection to justification does not stand. If his objection does not stand, then justification is at least vindicated from Plantinga's objection and may in fact be salvageable.

I want to conclude by arguing that Plantinga's objection to justification on the basis of proper function fails and that justification in the traditional sense, with the addition of true belief (and a "fillip to mollify Gettier"), is still necessary and (nearly) sufficient for knowledge. Justification may need a bit of work, but it does not need to be altogether rejected in favor of some other theory. Maybe justification can be described as having an appropriate reason for belief. Where an appropriate reason for belief is one that comes by means of a cognitive faculty functioning fully (reason used critically), without negligence, or misinterpretation, through the use of an argument (use of reason) or some other highly-probable evidence (perceptual, testimony, memory, etc.) as a means of support for true belief. Call this the carefulness criteria for justification.

The carefulness criteria is an opportunity to exercise the intellectual virtues, habits of mind that we have some control over, may cultivate, and for which we are responsible. These virtues may include intellectual humility, patience, diligence, and love of the truth. If we are able to know the truth, because our cognitive faculties do not malfunction, we ought to know the truth. If we love the truth, we will pursue the truth until we possess knowledge.

In retaining the classic definition of knowledge we could also propose that justification comes in degrees ranging from strong justification to weak justification. Strong justification is a sound argument, a necessary conclusion, that leads to certainty. Weak justification is based upon perceptual evidence that leads to a high probability of truth, such as in scientific claims. Justified true belief, with the addition of something like the carefulness criterion, would then be a proposed definition of knowledge.

[1]Plantinga, Alvin. *Warrant the Current Debate*. (New York: Oxford University Press, 1993), 6.
[2]Ibid., 100.
[3]Copi, Irving M. and Carl Cohen. *Introduction to Logic*, tenth edition. (New Jersey: Prentice Hall, 1998), 389.
[4]Plantinga, Alvin. *Warrant and Proper Function*. (New York: Oxford University Press; 1993), 105.
[5]Ibid.
[6]Ibid.
[7]Plantinga, *WCD*, 4.
[8]Ibid.
[9]Ibid., 81.
[10]Ibid., 82.
[11]Ibid., 94.
[12]Ibid., 170.
[13]Ibid.
[14]Plantinga, *WPF*, 14.
[15]This example is taken from: Sacks, Oliver. *A Leg to Stand On*. (New York: Simon and Schuster, 1984).
[16]Plantinga, *WCD*, 134.
[17]Plantinga, Alvin. *Warranted Christian Belief*. (New York: Oxford University Press, 2000), 109.
[18]Ibid., 110.
[19]Plantinga, *WCD*, 134-135.
[20]Ibid., 135.
[21]Ibid.

[22] Ibid., 136.
[23] Ibid.
[24] Ibid., 137.
[25] Reid, Thomas. *Inquiry and Essays*. Ed. Keith Lehrer and Ronald Beanblossom. (Indiana: Bobbs-Merrill Company, Inc., 1975), 275.
[26] Ibid., 277.
[27] Kvanvig, Jonathan. *Warrant in Contemporary Epistemology*. (Maryland: Rowman & Littlefield Publishers, Inc., 1996), 25-26.
[28] Reid, 261.
[29] Ibid., 276.
[30] Plantinga, *WCD*, 102.
[31] Ibid., 103.
[32] Plantinga, *WCD*, 105.
[33] Ibid., 103.
[34] Ibid.
[35] Ibid.
[36] Ibid., 104.
[37] Ibid., 105.
[38] Plantinga, *WPF*, 42.
[39] Ibid., 42-43.
[40] Ibid., 48.
[41] Ibid., 4.
[42] Ibid., 4.
[43] Ibid.
[44] Reid, xxv.
[45] Ibid.
[46] Pojman, Louis. *The Theory of Knowledge: Classic & Contemporary Readings*. (California: Wadsworth, Inc., 1993), 318.

Bibliography

Anderson, Owen. *The Clarity Of God's Existence: The Ethics of Belief After the Enlightenment* Oregon: Wipf & Stock, 2008.

BonJour, Laurence. *The Structure of Empirical Knowledge.* Cambridge: Harvard University Press, 1985.

Burton, Kelly. *Retrieving Knowledge: A Socratic Response to Skepticism.* Phoenix: Public Philosophy Press, 2018.

Copi, Irving M. and Carl Cohen. *Introduction to Logic*, tenth edition. New Jersey: Prentice Hall, 1998

Kvanvig, Jonathan. *Warrant in Contemporary Epistemology.* Maryland: Rowman & Littlefield Publishers, Inc., 1996.

Plantinga, Alvin. *Warrant: The Current Debate.* New York: Oxford University Press, 1993.

_____. *Warrant and Proper Function.* New York: Oxford University Press, 1993.

_____. *Warranted Christian Belief.* New York: Oxford University Press, 2000.

_____. "Reason and Belief in God." *Faith and Rationality: Reason and Belief in God*. Ed. Alvin Plantinga and Nicholas Wolterstorff. Indiana: University of Notre Dame Press, 1983.

Pojman, Louis. *The Theory of Knowledge: Classic & Contemporary Readings*. California: Wadsworth, Inc., 1993.

Reid, Thomas. *Inquiry and Essays*. Ed. Keith Lehrer and Ronald Beanblossom. Indiana: Bobbs-Merrill Company, Inc., 1975.

Also by Kelly Fitzsimmons Burton

Kelly Fitzsimmons Burton, Ph.D. has been a college Philosophy professor in Phoenix, AZ since 2003. She desires to see a new direction in contemporary philosophy that leads away from skepticism and towards knowledge. She enjoys reading Plato and arguing with Nietzsche. Kelly loves philosophical conversation and regularly engages in public philosophy. When not teaching or conversing, Kelly enjoys time with her husband and two cattle dogs in the Arizona desert. You may find more about Kelly's work on her website: http://retphi.com

Retrieving Knowledge: A Socratic Response to Skepticism

Retrieving Knowledge: A Socratic Response to Skepticism is an exercise in retrieval philosophy, using philosophical principles from the past to address contemporary challenges. The book begins with first philosophy's search for a logos, a source of explanation of the order and rationality in the world, and the failure to ground the logos in being. The story picks up with the skepticism of the Sophists and Socrates' attempt to address the epistemological and metaphysical sources of the skepticism of his day in Plato's dialogue Theaetetus.

Through this dialogue, we come to grapple with the definition of knowledge and the problems inherent with first philosophy's materialism. Knowledge is defined as a true belief with a logos (or an account). The theme of the logos is continued from first philosophy to Socrates and then to the Modern period of philosophy where we encounter a similar skepticism that Socrates addresses, a skepticism arising from metaphysical naturalism and empiricism. The moderate naturalism and empiricism of the Modern philosophers become the radical naturalism and empiricism of Nietzsche and the post-Nietzschean philosophers. The radical naturalism and empiricism of the post-Nietzschean philosophers lead to a contemporary negative nihilism carried out by the continental postmodernists, and a positive nihilism carried out by the Pragmatists and the "willing out beyond" of new values after Nietzsche's transvaluation of all values.

Retrieval of the arguments of Socrates from the Theaetetus is used to address contemporary skepticism in the same way that Socrates addressed the skepticism of his day. Post-Nietzschean philosophy poses challenges beyond what Socrates faced; thus, a new direction for the future of philosophy is needed. The epilogue provides a blueprint for how the original search for the logos as the heart of philosophy may continue today.

www.ingramcontent.com/pod-product-compliance
Lightning Source LLC
Chambersburg PA
CBHW021958290426
44108CB00012B/1118